A Coming Home For Me

Aili Jarvenpa

ACKNOWLEDGEMENTS

"Aunt Lydia,,"
"Taormina,"
"News Bulletin,"
"Mother Dream" and
"To Grandmother's House"
were all originally published by
North Star Press of St. Cloud, Inc.,
St. Cloud, Minnesota.

ISBN Number
0-9632975-8-9

Copyright © Aili Jarvenpa
1994

Published by
Sampo Publishing Co., Inc.
Box 120804
New Brighton, MN 55112

A Coming Home For Me

Contents

The Early Years:
A Coming Home For Me 1
Introduction 2
The "Finn Hall" Finns 4
Over The Meadow 7
Christmas Eve 11

The Relatives:
Cousin Hilma And Her Red Roses 13
Ancestral Fires 17
Aunt Lydia 18
Aunt Cecilia (The Isinglass Window) 20
Grandpa John 22
Mother Dream 26

Essays:
House Of Ghosts 28
The Generations 30
A Different View 31

Travel:
Hotel Villas Telamar 33
Hi-Jacked In Stockholm 34
To Grandmother's House 37
Off To Bayhead We Go 38
Our Trip West 40

Fiction:
The Middle Years 44
Avery Hall 50

Humor:
South of South Is North 58
A Matter Of Color 59
To My Old Friend 60
Oh Margaret 61
The Crazy World of Linguistics 62
April Blizzard 63
Four Eyes 64
Star Dust 65

Translations From The Finnish:
I Heard Women Singing 66
Silver and Violet 68
Life's Refugee 69
Chance 70
The Brides 71

Poetry And Prose:
The Taormina 75
Inner City High School 76
Dance Of The Snowshoe Hares 77
Three Years 78
News Bulletin 79
Kate Millett 80
My No Longer Child 80
The Spruce 81
Hymn To The Moon Goddess 82
Dream Of Aging 83
A Way Of Looking At The Sun 84
Arctic Tern 84
Invitation To Reunion 85
From Helsinki to Kennedy Airport 86
Day Of Reckoning 87

DEDICATION

I dedicate this book
in memory of my husband,
Oliver Jarvenpa.
As a wildlife biologist
for over thirty years,
he had studied every lake
and stream in Minnesota.

A Coming Home For Me

Fall Lake
Winton, Minnesota

>Luminous at sunrise,
it extends out before me,
past tall pines,
through light shadows of birches,
shimmering beyond the fringes of dawn.
The wind stirs, ripples the water,
whispers secrets of beginnings,
of French voyageurs
who passed this way long ago.
>
>It is a coming home for me,
to my north country lake
that waits for me at the end of the road,
serene and sparkling at daybreak,
yet rugged as the roar of its waterfall.
>
>Once the province of the lumberjack,
its waters, its virgin forests,
extend through boundaries,
through time.
>
>Finnish immigrants, our parents,
knew the ways of these waters,
ways learned in the old country,
knew the power of renewal here,
how it eased the longing for home.
>   This haven, to which I return,
>   Again and again.

INTRODUCTION

During my early childhood, Finnish was my only language, as was true of many children of Finnish immigrants. Many years later, after having studied Finnish immigrant culture and Finnish American culture, and having collected many of my writings during my many years on this planet, I find myself overwhelmed by the diversity of my memories, beginning shortly after the end of World War I, when I was three years old.

It was the period when the immigrants from Finland were rushing here. They had heard that they could get jobs on the Iron Range in Minnesota. They also had heard that the area was very similar to Finland, with its lakes and forests.

Among those immigrants was my father, who came in 1909. My mother arrived in 1913. They did not know each other until they met in Winton, Minnesota, where they were married in 1916. The village of Winton was actually a sawmill town, and many of the men, including my father, preferred to work in the sawmills rather than in the dangerous mines.

Winton was on the edge of what is now called the Boundary Waters, beginning with Fall Lake. In those early years, our Finnish community in Winton and Fall Lake were all I knew of this world. Until the age of four, I lived in a closely knit village where every one knew every one else, where every family had a summer cottage at Fall Lake, and where everyone spoke only Finnish, or so it seemed to me then.

Actually there were other ethnic groups in Winton, as I learned later. But in those early years,

My parents and I.

each group seemed to keep to themselves. That was so until the immigrant children were old enough to go to school and learn English and eventually get out into the "bigger" world.

My small family of three moved to Cloquet, Minnesota, a larger town, when I was four years old. It was a necessity since the sawmills in Winton were closing up. I began kindergarten in Cloquet at the age of five. The first day my teacher discovered that I didn't know a single word of English. It was not uncommon among immigrant children in those years, especially if you were an only child and didn't have an older brother or sister who had already learned English in school. I happened to be an only child. First grade turned out better for me. By the end of that school year, English had become my first language. Although I didn't realize it at the time, I had become bilingual!

Obviously the early experiences of immigrant children were quite different from those who grew up in homes where English was the main language. The immigrant child faced many complexities growing up. However, I believe those difficulties strengthened us. I now realize that it was a very rich learning experience that I will always value.

This book, A COMING HOME FOR ME, contains many of my writings that I have collected through the years, including prose, poetry, essays, short stories, translations from the Finnish, travel, and humor. It will take the reader to several places and happenings. Since I have lived most of my life in an American culture and have rediscovered my heritage as a Finnish American, these writings reflect my experiences.

My Mother, Aunt Cecelia and her son Toivo.

THE "FINN HALL" FINNS

My parents, both Finnish immigrants, were "Finn Hall" Finns, and that meant, of course, that I was too. All members of a family usually were active. Every age was involved. To this day I consider myself privileged to have been a part of that special phenomenon of the early decades of this century, that magic circle that is now gone. That is what it was - a magic circle that spread itself out over a big extended family.

The Finn Hall in Cloquet, Minnesota, offered fellowship and opportunities for making lasting friendships. It was a haven for the lonely immigrant adjusting to a new land. It offered music, drama, poetry. We attended variety programs, plays, dances, anniversary celebrations, weddings, funerals. We had youth clubs, a women's society, a library. We had lectures, debates. We had athletic programs for men and women. We had summer camps for children. We had instruction in Finnish. We had summer festivals in the city park. And did we have food! Dinners, lunches, picnics. And always coffee and pulla.

When a program or play was scheduled, and the curtain opened and the lights dimmed, I was transported into a world of fantasy. I was mesmerized when I watched Dorothy Sahlman perform a solo dance. To me she and her costumes were always so beautiful, and I am sure that others thought so too. Today we are impressed by the talents of her actress daughter, Jessica Lange.

The older children, ten to fifteen, who attended programs and plays, would usually stick together and hurry to fill up the first two or three rows. We would giggle and chatter in anticipation. When the lights dimmed, several voices would be heard saying, "hush," "hush." They were directed specifically at us. During intermission, when the adults were served their evening coffee and pulla, we children would sometimes skip the soda pop and run as fast as we could to the Tulip Shop on Cloquet Avenue to purchase candy bars. We would rush back breathlessly, just in time to sit down before the curtain went up again.

The choice of stage settings for plays was somewhat limited by what was available. If it was an outdoor scene, the backdrop was a rural setting of trees and grass and, if my memory serves me right, a cow grazing. But if it was an outdoor city scene, it was always the one of a street lined with tall buildings on both sides and a street lamp. A sophisticated farce about the rich was performed with terrific believability by these Finnish immigrants and their grown children turned actors. The stage setting, if it was a living room, was furnished to portray the proper opulence! They were truly creative, ingenious theater people. Two of the Cloquet Finn Hall theater directors were Väinö Lindfors and Nestor Petman.

The activities that occurred at the Cloquet Finn Hall were typical of those of numerous Finn Halls in Finnish immigrant communities in Minnesota and other states where Finnish immigrants settled. It would not be at all surprising, for example, to learn that the well known operetta, "Tukkijoella" (At Log River), might have been performed in Gardner, Massachusetts, around the same time as it was performed at the Cloquet Finn Hall in 1935. One of the Cloquet members, Elma Kuusisto, recently told me that their troupe also went on tour with the operetta, including a long, cold, winter drive in an unheated truck to Ironwood, Michigan. That was true commitment and dedication.

I still remember the year that a Finnish theater group from New York City performed at our hall. During intermission, several of us children who were beside ourselves with excitement managed to "sneak" upstairs from the back of the hall and then run down a corridor to the costume and make-up rooms. We were, of course, quite awed and impressed by what seemed to us the incredible sophistication and worldliness of these New York actors and actresses— better than movie stars! They, in turn, talked and laughed with us, teased us, put us at ease. In fact, they seemed pleased at our intrusion!

Perhaps the most embarrassing moment of my life happened at the Finn Hall when I was about eleven or twelve. I had been studying the violin for perhaps two or three years and was still quite unsure of myself. But as at all Finn Halls, children were invited and encouraged to take part in the programs. With some reluctance I agreed to play a violin solo at a forthcoming spring program.

The eventful evening finally arrived. I got panicky when I peered through a small hole in the stage curtain and saw that all the rows on the main floor and also the balcony were filling up rapidly. Then there was the agonizing wait for my turn on the program. Individual solo numbers were usually presented from a small balcony off to the side of the stage. I eventually found myself standing there playing a violin piece, the name of which I have mercifully forgotten. As I played, my eyes were glued to the sheet of music on the music stand.

Suddenly I heard an awful sound that did not stop, a sort of howling sound as though the whole audience was mocking me. I froze, then turned and ran through the door leading back of the curtain. It wasn't until several minutes later that I learned that a dog had sneaked into the hall. He had followed his owner, a teen-aged boy who didn't realize his dog was there until it began to howl! It was little comfort for me to know it was a dog rather than the audience that had jeered me. In my embarrassment and misery, I was sure that the dog was an expert music critic!

Dances were frequently scheduled at the hall. It was always packed on such evenings, and the music was sure to start your feet a-tapping. Immigrant parents brought their children, who learned the joys of ballroom dancing at an early age. The popular Beany Saltvik Band played often. There was much excitement whenever Viola Turpeinen with her accordion included Cloquet in her dance tour. Then she married Bill Syrjala, a talented violinist and native of Cloquet. Their music filled our hall many times.

I have often thought that I was influenced becoming a poet because I heard so much poetry presented at the Finn Hall and at the summer festivals. Poetry was definitely a very important part of every program. For example, I have a copy of a program for the summer festival held in Ishpeming, Michigan in August 1938. The program lists four poetry readings, of which one is a special festival poem written especially for that occasion and two readings are poems read together by the entire audience!

In an article that I wrote, "Twentieth Century Finnish American Poetry," for a conference, Finn Forum III, held in Turku, Finland in September 1984, I quote Taimi Johnson, a second generation Finnish American:

> **Back in the 'twenties and 'thirties, there was a program every Sunday evening at the Finn Hall in my hometown, Crosby, Minnesota, which always included music (vocal and instrumental), a poem, and a speech.**
>
> **The poem was important. The reader spoke the lines with emotion and with almost exaggerated expression.**
>
> **I shall always remember a program I attended at the Kenttä Haali in Lake Worth, Florida, in the 1960's. A frail, elderly man, assisted by a cane and a friend, slowly and with great effort managed to maneuver onto the stage, where a transformation occurred. His light body straightened, and an inner strength emanated from him, as in clear well-modulated tones he recited from memory, with beautiful expression, a long poem of dozens of verses. I was impressed, literally moved to tears.**

Yes, there are a few, but very few, Finn Halls left in this country. Kenttä Haali is still functioning in Lake Worth, Florida, but the members are mostly senior citizens. In fact, my father, who retired to Lake Worth, had a role in several plays at the Kenttä Haali in the 'sixties and early 'seventies. I understand that there is still a hall in Berkeley, California. Most of the Finn Halls, however, remain now only in our memories. Such rich memories.

Over The Meadow ...

...and through the woods
to Grandmother's house
we go...

The children in Miss Brown's fourth grade class at Garfield School in Cloquet, Minnesota, would sing the above words with great excitement back in 1927. And why shouldn't we? Thanksgiving would soon be here. The classroom was decorated for the special holiday with our drawings of Pilgrims and turkeys. Our teacher and our books had told us that this was a time to be happy and thankful. And what could be more fun than going to Grandma's on Thanksgiving? Everybody would be there. All the cousins. And we kids could play in the hayloft. Then there would be all that food. The big table would be groaning with all the dishes cooked by Grandmother, Mother and the aunts.

A lovely, nostalgic picture, but was it entirely true? Is it true now? More often than not, today's young families find themselves separated from the rest of their relatives. Work cannot always be found where the family settled originally. The "company" moves to another state and takes the family with them. Father is laid off when the factory or mine closes for good, and there is no choice but to look for work elsewhere. Tearful goodbyes are said to Grandma with promises to come home for Thanksgiving or Christmas, promises that cannot always be kept. That scenario is apt to be repeated many times now, and we look back and sigh for the good old days when families lived close together.

In the 1920's there were big extended families with grandmothers and grandfathers and uncles and aunts and dozens of cousins nearby. If Grandma happened to live next door, a child could run over to her for comforting any time, or down the street a short way to Aunt Lil's. It seemed like a very secure, safe world in which a child could grow up — those early decades of this century.

Was it really the "good old days"? I am sure it was — for some, that is. Especially for those living in the established, small rural communities in the years when our country was more rural than urban. But was it usually for that way for the immigrants? For the Finnish immigrants? Each of my parents came here alone from Finland. They met in northeastern Minnesota where so many immigrants came. I never knew my grandparents. My paternal grandmother died in Finland when Father was only ten years old, my paternal grandfather in 1922. My maternal grandfather also died in the early 1920's. A letter edged in black arrived in the spring of 1936 just as we were making plans to sail to Finland that very summer to visit my maternal grandmother. My mother was devastated. Of course the trip was cancelled.

In 1927, when I was anticipating Thanksgiving and singing "To Grandmother's House" in fourth grade, I had a lump in my throat because throughout my childhood and into adulthood I have had this feeling of something missing that should be a natural part of childhood, of growing up — participation in the natural continuance of the generations. Not just letters from a faraway land across the seas written in a language not easily accessible to a child of immigrants. Not just photographs to look at and wonder about.

Of course it was painfully hard for the immigrants to leave their parents, their brothers and sisters, knowing full well it might be forever. We, their children born here, did not experience that pain. Our pain was a different kind of pain — more of a void, an emptiness that could never be filled. If the realization did not dawn on us before, it certainly did in grade school when we sang songs about going to Grandmother's house and hear our more Americanized classmates chatter excitedly about their Grandmas and Grandpas.

The uniqueness of the immigrant experience as it has touched each of the first three generations — the immigrant (first generation), the child of the

Thanksgiving when I was in fourth grade, Cloquet, Minn.

immigrant born in this country (second generation), the grandchild of the immigrant (third generation Finnish-American) — came into sharper focus for me one summer when I participated in the Reunion of Sisters Conference at the University of Minnesota. The poetry written by granddaughters reveals the special close relationship between the immigrant grandmother and granddaughter with an added poignancy because of the language barrier. The poetry of the daughter of the immigrant mother may reveal confusion on the part of the daughter as she strives to live in two cultures, speaking English in school, Finnish at home. She may reveal the pressure the community and the school places on her to reject her heritage in order to become Americanized, a problem that is missing in the granddaughter's poetry since such pressure is no longer exerted by society. She is, therefore, free to express herself more openly, more honestly. Some immigrant poets, whose work I have translated, reveal their homesickness, their deep love for their children which they may have been too reticent to express verbally.

The place of the grandmother, the mummu, in the immigrant experience was given special emphasis at the Conference, as it should. I would like to share an excerpt from one of the poems written about Finnish immigrant grandmothers by their granddaughters.

Marcelle Doby Williams writes about her grandmother in an excerpt from her poem, "Edge of Winter":

> In northern Wisconsin, on a small farm
> Taken with difficulty from sand and pine wilderness
> My grandmother awakens.
>
> She, one of many hungered for a new land,
> and being one of many, her stride was strong,
> As steady as hoof beats:
>
> the mixing spoon on the bowl,
> the hoe as it felled the weeds,
> the snap of carpets in the wind
> as old dust was hurled into the horizon.

I, like most other Finnish-American children of immigrants, could have spoken Finnish with my grandmother if she had been here. In fact, I spoke only Finnish until I began to learn English when I started school. That, too, was a common experience for many children of immigrants.

I should mention that, while there were some children of immigrants who had grandparents in this country, they were very few. I knew personally of only three such families. Two aunts of my father, together with their husbands and children, grown and half-grown, had come to Minnesota from Finland at the very beginning of the century. The grown children had married here and had children of my age — my second cousins. They lived over a hundred miles from us, so we could not visit frequently in those days. When we did, I confess I was envious. How wonderful for my cousins to have their grandparents living right in the same block! Not in a faraway country with nothing but a faded photograph to look at.

For years, as a poet, I have felt a certain loss because I could never write a poem about my grandmother. I'm not sure exactly how the poem finally started to evolve. It probably just grew inside of me after one of my trips in Finland. That time I met all the relatives that lived in my mother's home, still standing there on a high hill. It was so wonderful to be there, to be warmly greeted, to see the pictures of Mother and her sisters on the living room wall, all of them now diseased. My cousin Hilja was so warm and caring. I kept growing younger and younger in her care. She became my grandmother.

Christmas Eve 1954

While there have been many Christmas Eves to look back upon with nostalgia, in retrospect, Christmas Eve of 1954 stands out for me as a special time of joy and innocence, one that can never quite be recaptured again. We were still young, Oliver and I, with two sons ages three and eight. We had much to be thankful for. And that year we looked forward to sharing part of the holidays with my parents. Plans were afoot for a gathering of the relatives at Mother's on Christmas Eve. In mid-afternoon, December 24, we piled into our year-old Plymouth, the four of us, the Christmas gifts hidden in the trunk, and left our home in Columbia Heights, heading north on Highway 61 toward Cloquet, my hometown.

The street lights were already on when we arrived at 1614 Carlton Avenue. They shined like stars on the freshly fallen snow. I noticed that Mother had placed candles at the front windows, as was her tradition on Christmas Eve, to guide a lost traveler who might be passing by. We went to the back door and entered the warm kitchen filled with enticing aromas. The table, set with a red cloth and candles, groaned with an array of traditional Finnish Christmas foods that Mother had baked and, of course, Father's special homemade head cheese and potato sausage.

The relatives began to arrive, carrying pumpkin pies and jello salads topped with mounds of whipped cream. The word "cholesterol" was unheard of then. Uncle David hung a beautiful Christmas wreath that he had made for our front door, and Uncle Otto brought some venison and homemade wine. Father was his usual energetic, talkative self. He urged everyone to help themselves to more food and coffee and passed around his usual Christmas box of chocolate covered cherries. Mother, in her quiet manner, managed to keep the table replenished, while the two aunts sliced pies and cakes and chattered happily.

When we saw the Christmas tree all lit up and in all its glory, we all oohed and aahed, and joined together in singing old familiar Christmas carols. Just as we had finished singing, there was a loud thump, thump at the front door, and I know that I heard sleigh bells. With a knowing smile, Father rushed to open the door.

In came Santa Claus as authentic looking as I had ever seen, carrying a big bag of gifts on his back. He was plump and jolly, and he "ho ho hoed" to the delight of the children, especially our three-year-old Alan. Later I learned that Santa was really Henry Mattson from up the street—good neighbor and Cloquet's newly elected legislator to the State Capitol. Undoubtedly it was a typical Christmas Eve, but for me it remains very special because it was my last Christmas Eve with Mother. She died unexpectedly of a heart attack the following September. She was 59.

Cousin Hilma and Her Red Roses

I had just turned fourteen when I met Cousin Hilma for the first time. Actually, she was Father's cousin. They had grown up in the same parish in Finland. Father often talked about the big house named Lusti, where Cousin Hilma grew up. She was eleven years younger than Father, but he remembered clearly the August day in 1909 when, at eighteen, he said good-by to seven-year-old Cousin Hilma and left alone to America. His destination was a place called Winton, Minnesota, where his oldest sister, Arma, had emigrated two years before.

Cousin Hilma, being so much younger, didn't arrive in America until 1922. What excited me, as an impressionable teenager, was to learn that she had chosen to live in New York City. What could be more glamorous, I thought.

Cousin Hilma surprised our family by arriving at our door step without earlier notice on a July afternoon in 1933. She was dressed to the nine's in a fashionable suit, carrying a fur piece thrown casually over her left arm and clutching two dozen of the most beautiful long stemmed red roses I had ever seen, not to mention her pearl necklace, high-heeled black patent leather pumps, and her lovely blond hair waved in the latest fashion. You rarely saw such a sight in our living room.

Cousin Hilma and I.

I was so glad that Father had bought the maroon colored mohair couch and matching chairs the year before the depression set in. Mother had recently crocheted a lovely lace doily for the small mahogany table in the center of the living room, on which sat the big family album in its maroon velvet cover. Mother's plants had started to bloom, and the imitation oriental rug on the floor could almost pass for the real thing, I thought. Oh, how I hoped that Cousin Hilma would think that Father had done well in America too. Father and Cousin Hilma were oblivious to everyone else as they tried to catch up on all the news. But suddenly Father looked up and gave his famous signal to Mother: it's time to put the coffee pot on. I always noticed his signal, but guests never did. It was a characteristic lifting of his left eyebrow and an almost indiscernible movement of his head toward the kitchen. In our home it was Father who decided when the guests should be served, the Finnish coffee ritual of course being very special. In Father's opinion, the timing for it should be just right, just at the time when the conversation was still interesting but in possible danger of waning a bit. Coffee time was a perfect change of pace, a good time to relax, to enjoy the food and drink, and to resurrect past happenings and tell stories.

Many years passed by before I saw Cousin Hilma again. Sometimes I would think about her and her life in New York City, so far away from my home in Cloquet, Minnesota. Mother and Father would keep contact with her by letter. But it wasn't until I grew up and was living in Washington D.C., just before World War II began, that Cousin Hilma entered my life again. I was engaged to be married, and Cousin Hilma was delighted. She had a lot to do with our wedding plans. After a small wedding in Washington D.C., since we didn't have many close friends nearby, we then followed Cousin Hilma's suggestion that we go to New York City for our honeymoon.

So off to New York we went. Cousin Hilma had made many arrangements for us, including a room for us in one of the best hotels in the city. The day after our arrival she appeared at our door with an armful of two dozen long-stemmed red roses. It triggered my memory of the red roses she brought to my family years ago. I almost cried. It was such a sweet gesture.

It was way back in 1941, but I will never forget our honeymoon in Manhattan. My young husband and I were not prepared for all the excitement planned for us by Cousin Hilma and her boyfriend, Justin Lauga. Justin, who was originally from Paris, was the chauffeur for the President of the American Woolen Company. Somehow Justin got permission to use his limousine. And so we were driven in high style all over Manhattan: to Times Square, Radio City Music Hall, Rockefeller Center, Broadway, Chinatown and so on and so on. Justin, a delightful person, had a brother, also from Paris, who worked as a maitre d' in a French restaurant. We were taken there for a beautiful evening that I will always remember.

Not long after our honeymoon, World War II began. My husband had to join the army. He went overseas and I returned to Minnesota. After his four years overseas, we were finally able to get our family together. Cousin Hilma and I resumed our correspondence after the war ended. Meanwhile, after all our three children were old enough to travel, we often traveled as a family to the East Coast where my husband had many relatives in New Jersey. And almost every visit included a visit to Manhattan to see Cousin Hilma. Those trips were especially exciting for us because Cousin Hilma knew just where to direct us to special places in the Big Apple.

We usually met Cousin Hilma at whatever hotel we were staying at the time. But on one occasion she insisted inviting us to her apartment. That is when we discovered that she was a housekeeper (or a "domestic" you could say) who worked for a very rich woman who lived in an elegant apartment. She was so rich that she was listed in the "Blue Book". In fact the "Blue Book" was on her living room table, indicating that she was one of the very richest New Yorkers. The "500" they call them.

Cousin Hilma called her "Her Lady" . "Her Lady" often went on vacations to the mountains or the seashore in the summer. And that very day we learned that

Cousin Hilma, me, cousin Ella in top row. The children: Leona, Robert and Alan. Pictured in New York City.

"Her Lady" was on her way to the seashore, to stay there for several weeks. That, I believe is why Cousin Hilma was able to invite us to her apartment, which was really "Her Lady's" apartment. We began to realize that Cousin Hilma was a servant who lived and worked in the apartment almost every day, often around the clock, with one day off each week. The apartment was beautiful, and she had prepared a delicious luncheon for us, with most of the food arranged on silver plates and a centerpiece of lovely flowers — yes, red roses of course.

After lunch Cousin Hilma took us on a tour of the entire apartment. Then, rather quietly, she opened a door to what she said was her bedroom. I was shocked. It was a very small, narrow room, where there was hardly any room to turn around: a narrow single bed, a wooden chair, a mirror on the wall, and a small chest that she must have brought from Finland.

In those years, many young women emigrated from Finland and remained on the East Coast where they could get jobs as domestics. One of the things I have learned was that immigrant domestics were not allowed to get married. For example, "Her Lady" never met Justin. Eventually Justin married Cousin Hilma, but it was kept a secret.

We continued to keep in touch with Cousin Hilma. After some years she moved to Massachusetts to be near relatives. She had begun to have health problems.

In the summer of 1978 I had a phone call from Florida that my father had died. He had lived in Florida for over twenty years. He was getting old, but we weren't prepared for his passing away as yet. I hurried around to arrange the trip to his funeral in Florida. My husband had just injured his leg, but my daughter offered to go with me. On arrival, I suddenly remembered that I hadn't phoned Cousin Hilma about my Father's death. I rushed to the phone and managed to get the message through. She was saddened by the news, of course, and asked me if I would arrange for red roses at my Father's funeral. Of course I said "yes". Since I had told her that I was going to Finland in August, she also asked me if I would place flowers at her parents' graves.

My daughter and I had been home for about five days when the phone rang. It was an unfamiliar voice telling me that Cousin Hilma had died. I was so sad. First Father, then Cousin Hilma. But we went to Finland, as we had planned, and when we got to Kangasniemi in August, I placed an armful of red roses on her parents' graves, as Cousin Hilma had requested.

Ancestral Fires

Days grow shorter.
December darkness moves in.
I light candles,
wrap a shawl around my shoulders.
I begin to chant,
form words in the language of my childhood,
wrap my tongue around half-forgotten syllables
of an ancient language:

      Mieleni minun tekevi   (It is my wish,
      aivoni ajattelevi   it is my desire,
      lähteäni laulamahan   to begin singing,
      laulamahan surustani. to sing about my sorrow.)

I recall early years of childhood,
sad songs immigrant women sang in our village.
Now I sing songs of sadness,
of the heavy cloud hovering over us.
Every winter it foretells news of yet another loss,
black-edged letter on its way from the homeland,
young mother's death in the cold of a Minnesota winter.
Through long winter months, winter nights,
our northern legacy of melancholy envelops us.

Winter, slowly, reluctantly, blends into spring.
At last June arrives—the summer solstice!
Myriads of rainbows transform me.
I dance across green meadows,
weave garlands for my hair.
I laugh. I sing.

Juhannus aatto! (Midsummer's Eve!)
There is magic in the air!
Sun-magic, Moon-Magic!
No sorrow, no darkness tonight!

From across continents, oceans,
my blood connects with ancestral fires,
fires that burn tonight on distant lakes and hills.

AUNT LYDIA
(February 19, 1894 - May 18, 1973)

I

As so many springs before,
the May morning awakened her
with the scent of apple blossoms,
brought color to her thin pale cheeks,
a lilt to her halting step.

She hung freshly laundered curtains,
diaphanous white,
at the kitchen window,
turned a patch of earth
for a garden, a garden
that now grows somewhere
beyond our vision.

She smiled as she set the table
with her best cups and saucers
edged with wreaths of painted roses.

The day's tasks well done,
she lay down for a nap,
her softly tinted hair in curlers
so she'd look nice for her coffee party.

Her first guest,
uninvited,
entered quietly.

II

Today I mourn, and I wonder
what thoughts were yours, Aunt Lydia,
behind that quiet, stoic manner
with which you faced
the harshest turns of life.

What were they when,
at seventeen,
you sailed here from a home
where hunger was a daily guest,
Where your young, strong mother
died in childbirth

after slipping on the icebound river
on her way to church in winter,
your devout mother, who had couched you
until verse after Bible verse
spilled from your childish lips
without an error?

Is that when you lost your childhood faith,
when she left you when you were seven,
left your brothers and your sisters,
left your father,
too old and ill to be a father?

Or was it here that you set
the old hymns and prayers aside,
those early years
when the robber barons of the Vermilion Range
seduced unwary immigrants,
your young husband,
down into their underground mines,
mines ruthlessly mined,
vermilion ore veined,
vermilion blood stained,
blacklisted those who dared protest,
imported new innocents to take their place.

III

You are the essence of the past. Widowed,
you lived alone in your small house with its
paper flowers in vases. Paper flowers, pink
and gold and lavender, turned not toward the
sun but toward the past. And not one paper
flower ever gathered dust. No lace curtain
ever wilted. And no floor ever dared stop
shining.

You would welcome us with food that set us
groaning. And you would always say goodbye
by firmly pressing in my hand a loaf of warm
rye bread or a glass of wild blueberry jam.
I remember how you and I would tend my mother's
grave each May. Today I tend yours. And as
I quench their thirst, I see the flowers turn
their faces toward the sun.

The Isinglass Window

(A True Story)

We have come to Winton, Minnesota from all directions to pay homage to an extraordinary woman. We have come from the East Coast, the West Coast, from Minneapolis and St. Louis. We have come from northeastern towns of Minnesota, from Ely, Hibbing, Tower, and Duluth. Undoubtedly some of us still remember how, as children, we would stand before her, tongue-tied, awed by her presence.

We fill the Winton Village Hall to bursting as we gather together after the funeral, share memories over coffee, reminisce about her vibrant life of eighty-eight years. Yes, we have all come today — her two sons, their spouses, the grandchildren and great-grandchildren and, of course, other relatives and friends by the score.

I knew her as Father's cousin and as the wife of my mother's brother, Uncle Toivo. But I knew her best as Aunt Cecilia, a person to admire, a person not to be reckoned with.

On this day, March 13, 1984, winter is slowly beginning to loosen a grip on Winton, a northeastern Minnesota village not far from the boundary waters, from Canada. Fall Lake, bordering Winton, is still frozen. Once a raw, bustling sawmill town, immigrants knew then that they had a good chance of finding work in Winton, and they soon learned who would help them find it.

Winton's old wooden sidewalks, long since gone, still echo Aunt Cecilia's brisk walk when, as a teenager, she led shy young Finnish immigrant men, barely off the boat, to the employment office of the St. Croix Lumber Company, and translated their whispered Finnish into clearly enunciated English.

Aunt Cecilia was born feisty. She had opinions, strong opinions, usually very well considered. And she seldom kept them to herself. There were times when strong men would stammer, turn red-faced in her presence, either from embarrassment or frustration. As one of my uncles once said, not wanting to believe that any woman could know so much about the world situation, "Well, Cecilia can't know everything." But he made sure that she didn't hear what he said.

Aunt Cecilia had total recall. I can still hear her voice, strong and clear, as she told about the arrival of her father, and later of Aunt Cecilia and her mother from the old country:

> "Father came first in 1900. Then he sent for Mother and me. Mother sold our house in the city of Viipuri, and Mother and I arrived in America in March 1901. I was four years old. At Ellis Island they put Mother and me in a cage."

And how many times she liked to tell us about finally arriving at the Ely railroad station, four miles south of Winton:

"Father was there to meet us, and we were so happy to see him. And you'd never guess what I saw in that station. I thought it was the most beautiful thing in the world: a great big pot-bellied stove, one of those coal burning stoves, you know, with bright flames shining through the isinglass window. I decided that I would have a stove just like that some day."

It didn't take long for Aunt Cecilia and her parents to settle into their new home in Winton, where her father found work at the sawmill, nor was it long before their home had a pot-bellied stove with an isinglass window.

Aunt Cecilia had always been drawn to bright lights, and as she grew older she often had the female lead in plays at the Winton Finn Hall, and then on tour to iron range towns, and even to Duluth: in Minna Canth's "Workman's Wife", in Moliere's "The Miser," and in "Log River," among others. And then there were the plays she would translate into Finnish: "Charley's Aunt" and "East Lynne," to name a few. She would dictate and Uncle Toivo would type scripts late into the night.

Toivo, Jr., Aunt Cecilia's older son, played the part of the nine-year-old boy who dies in the last act of "East Lynne," his first and last attempt at theater. But no one was too surprised when, around 1930, Aunt Cecilia went east to try her luck at New York City theater, just about the time when the depression was getting into full swing. She couldn't have picked a worse time. She returned home undaunted, head held high, knowing full well some tongues might be wagging,

We have come from all directions to honor and remember the four-year old immigrant girl who grew up to become a leader in the temperance movement, who organized a library for the Finnish immigrant community, the immigrant girl who, for a number of years, was a radio newscaster of local, national and world news in Finnish translation from radio stations in Ely, Hibbing, and Duluth, and who about 1960 directed a tour group of Finnish immigrants on a visit to their beloved homeland.

Widowed in her mid-fifties, Aunt Cecilia moved to Duluth and worked for a daily newspaper for a number of years. The last decade of her life she lived at the Bloomenson Nursing Home in Ely, crippled by arthritis, weakened by leukemia. But she found ways to stay involved. She remained the storyteller, the visionary on top of all the latest news from the State Capitol, Washington, D.C., Finland, Beirut, Central America, wherever important news surfaced.

Grandpa John

Grandpa John, my husband's father, arrived last week from the East Coast to stay with us for a while. He flew alone from New York, his luggage mailed separately to simplify things for him. You see, he is 87 and cannot see too well, although his doctor says he will never go completely blind.

He has come to see us many times before, but it is different now. Perhaps for the first time in Grandpa John's life he doesn't know exactly where his home is or will be, or where he wants it to be; he, who has had so many homes, first as a child in the Old Country, then here.

Grandpa John, with his own hands, built homes on farms and in towns in northeastern Minnesota. When he was 65 years old, he built a home not far from the ocean in Florida, where he lived for about twenty years, and which he misses so much. He has built fancy houseboats for vacationers on northern lakes and huge ships for the Navy in California during World War II. As the years went by, things changed for him, first his home in Florida where his second wife died, and now his home with his daughter on the East Coast, where she is no longer well enough to take care of him.

Grandpa John is staying with us now while his oldest son and daughter-in-law are taking their first trip to Europe. They will be gone for a month and are planning to visit Grandpa's childhood home in Finland, the home he left sixty years ago and where two of his younger sisters still live, with a large extended family in the surrounding area. Grandpa John has been back to Finland only once. That was 25 years ago. His mind is still bright, his memory diamond sharp, and oh how much he would like to go with them. But now he is too old and frail.

Grandpa John's ties here in Minnesota also run deep, perhaps deepest here in the far northeastern corner of the state. And his next stop is among those who are left. His first wife is buried here—the bride of his youth, who died at 28 in the influenza epidemic, leaving him with four children, ages 3 to 9. He vowed to raise them alone until they were grown, a vow he kept. Their first home on the farm is long since gone. His older brother, his nearest neighbor, died ten years ago. His old friends are gone except for a few living out their last days in nursing homes. But there is a younger sister-in-law and brother-in-law and dozens of nieces and nephews and their children and their grandchildren. But it won't be the same. Their lives, too, have changed, and no place will seem like home.

Grandpa John was christened Johannes. While he speaks English quite well, he prefers his mother tongue whenever he is with those who understand and speak it. These weeks he has regaled me with tale after tale in his old provincial dialect.

A big man with a slight stoop and thinning hair, his manner is quiet and gentle, his face serene. He smiles easily. In the 38 years I have known him, I have never heard him speak a harsh word. Never has he tried to dictate to us how we should live our lives. He is the most accepting of men, and yet, if anyone has a right to rage at life, it is he. This past week I marveled at his serenity as he sat in the rocking chair and rocked and hummed and smiled to himself, his cane propped close by to aid his faltering step when he would get up and get a bit confused by the unfamiliar floor plan of our new home.

While my husband (Grandpa John's son) was working at his office, Grandpa John would share mid-morning and mid-afternoon coffee breaks with me, and we would chat together. Each day I would read to him the letters that arrived as well as daily news in the newspapers, since his vision was no longer clear. He, in turn, would relate with obvious relish, but with a touch of his usual shyness, many whimsical and often poignant tales from the past. His memory astounded me.

I knew he had had very little formal education as a child, but he had been a compulsive reader until his eyesight began to fail. Now his eyesight is so impaired he can no longer see even the big headlines in the daily newspaper.

He told me that he learned to read and write as a child from a circuit-riding teacher provided by the province. The instruction lasted exactly two

John Järvenpää and his sister in Finland.

weeks. The rest he learned by himself and from older brothers and sisters.

With much delight, he told me how, at fifteen, while attending confirmation for Lutheran Church membership, he sneaked away one day to see a performance in the nearby town of the great classic by Aleksis Kivi entitled Seven Brothers. He had read the novel several times and just couldn't bear to miss it. But he had to leave before it ended so his parents wouldn't suspect that he had played hookey from confirmation. He laughed as he remembered.

The next day, as we talked about children, he said, "It's very bad how adults frighten children with their foolish superstitions and fear of death and cemeteries." I nodded agreement. He added:

"I was afraid to go past cemeteries when I was little because of all the stories I heard grown ups tell. But then an old friend of my father's told me a story that helped me. He said that one evening when he was walking past a cemetery, and it was already getting dark, he heard what sounded like a small child crying. He stopped to listen, and he was sure it came from within the cemetery. He finally gathered up enough courage to go in through the gate. As he walked, the crying grew louder. He froze suddenly when it seemed that it was coming from a freshly prepared grave directly in front of him. He told me that he has been thankful that he didn't turn around then and run, although he certainly wanted to. He stooped down to listen, and as he did, he saw in the grass next to the grave a baby lamb which had strayed through an opening in the nearby fence dividing the cemetery from a farmer's pasture. The lost lamb was crying for its mother."

That evening Grandpa John, for the first and only time, alluded to some of the hardships he had had as a young man in a new country, trying to learn a new language — a young man of twenty with a young wife and a baby daughter. They lived in a crude, ugly mining town in northeastern Minnesota, named Sparta, the mine a dangerous, underground iron ore mine. He found that he had not come to the land of gold-lined streets as the brochures promised before he sailed to America, but iron ore in underground catacombs, catacombs filled with dust that choked and blinded when dynamite was set to blast loose the ore. Catacombs where only one shaft opening to the sky and to safety, did not provide enough air to light one candle. But the miners learned how to keep candles burning. By lighting two candles and leaning them against each other, they stayed lit. By using three together, the flame was bright.

As the intolerable conditions worsened, with no promise or hope of change, there was talk of a strike. Grandpa John said he dared to speak to the foreman about how dangerous the working conditions were. The foreman stared at him and said:

"John Boy, you have a young wife and baby don't you?" "Yes," he said. "Then you better watch out what you say around here."

Even before the foreman had finish speaking, Grandpa John had picked up his lunch pail and left the mine for good. Grandpa John slapped his knee and chuckled as he finished his tale about his career in the mine.

Then Grandpa John homesteaded a piece of land not far from the farm of his wife's parents. He built a home, cleared the land for farming, and when his wife died, he not only farmed, logged, hunted, trapped and fished to feed his family, but also baked bread and was both father and mother to four children until they were old enough to leave home. And he built and painted houses for others as well as himself. He remarried when the children were grown and built a home for his new wife, first in Minnesota, and later, when he was old enough to retire, a lovely home for them in Florida. He nursed his second wife with incomparable tenderness before she died of cancer a few years ago.

Now, after the month's visit with us, Grandpa John sits in the home of his oldest son in Duluth, rocking and humming and smiling as he sits and rocks, his cane propped nearby to help his faltering step in yet another house with a different floor plan. And in each home of his children that he visits, he becomes reacquainted with the many grandchildren who have matured, grown tall, some with children of their own, whom he quickly accepts and loves. All have more formal education than

John Järvenpää and daughter Ella Nurmi saying goodbye on the boat.

Grandpa John. Some are teachers, some university professors, but none claim that they know as much as Grandpa John.

I am sure that many times this week he laughs, shoulders shaking, as he tells tales of hope and of escapades from a life so hard that we wonder how he ever made it. And we wonder how he has such peace of mind when he doesn't even know for sure where home is now.

(Grandpa John died peacefully in Duluth in August 1977, with his family at his side.)

Mother Dream

I

I roll dough out on the board
cut three strands
Never get them even like Mother did
Braid three uneven strands
smelling of cardamom into coffee bread

Braid, braid Mother's long hair
divide it in three
Weave one thick braid
down her back for the night
her back bent in her last illness

A dark strand
escaping awkward fingers
flows out over darkness
I reach out to gather it
flowing over water
edge of madness
waters black in shadows of the spruce
no stars to show the way

She cannot breathe
I cannot breathe for her
I cannot breathe
I run, escape
to another room, and another

none familiar
one leading to another
leading nowhere.

A strange door opens toward the lake
I hear water lap against
an old boat moored near shore
feel oars in my hands
smell dankness of the wood
fish smell of the last catch
death smell
row back and forth,
rock back and forth, back and forth
going nowhere
nowhere

II
I cradle myself
in this lonely ark
breathe in
the salt of the sea
I mother myself
to the sound of the surf
to the cry of the gulls
flying near.

Cradled, I sleep
in this lonely ark,
rock to the throb
of the sea,
healing waters
rush through my bones
washing, washing
the wounds of my grief.

I rock
                I sleep
I rock
                I sleep

sleep in the arms
of the mother,
sleep in the arms
of the sea.

House of Ghosts

You insist on living with me, Finnish Ghost of winter wars, of famines that I've only read about, ghost from the land of the midnight sun, from the land of my parents' birth.

I have been afraid to tell you that my home may not be right for you. Yes, my eyes get misty when I see your flag, blue on white, flying in the sunlight. And I am moved when I hear your national anthem:

> *"Oi Maamme, Suomi, synnyin maa*
> *soi sana kultainen!..."*

Oh, yes, I speak your language, and Father and Mother also taught me to read and write Finnish. I sing in it, dream in it, love in it, rage in it. I am enraptured by your Kalevala, its superb collection of legends of Finnish mythology rooted in the hearts of your people; its poetry and runes sung down through the ages; its heroes, Väinämöinen, Lemminkäinen, Ilmarinen. I remember the tale of the majestic swan floating and singing on a dark river surrounding Tuonela, the Hades of your folk lore. This somber legend is so richly portrayed by your famous composer, Jean Sibelius, in his musical composition, "Swan of Tuonela." I remember as a child trying to play Sibelius' "Valse Triste" on my violin. I was too young then to comprehend or interpret a woman's dance with death. I am especially moved by Sibelius' powerful symphonic work, "Finlandia," which he composed for a tableaux of historical and legendary scenes and, which for me, is the ultimate creative expression of what your country is.

But you should know much more about me, my Finnish Ghost, before you decide whether you should stay. I don't have much intestinal fortitude, that essential Finnish trait you call sisu. I am not brave. I am afraid of bears and heights and many other things. After a hot sauna, I have never jumped into a cold lake through a hole chopped in the ice, and I know I never will.

I am not stoic. I laugh easily, cry easily, and talk too much. I even talk with my hands. Sometimes I'm as demonstrative as the Italians, and I'm drawn to the charm of the Irish. So don't lay any labels on me, Ghost.

Furthermore, I don't go along with your fetish for cleanliness. I refuse to spend all my days chasing dust. But I am literate, and I read a lot. Ah! A smile of approval! But I'm not as frugal as you, although I do pay my debts promptly. Yes, and sometimes I spend money on things you might consider frivolous. Please don't frown that way.

Also, you must know that in my house are other ghosts. They are from the land of my birth, from our wars, our hungry years. The ghosts of the Native American, of the Black American, of the children who died in ghettos — they all live with me. I am haunted by the generations of women who were too weary or too regimented to question why the Bill of Rights didn't apply to them. I am haunted by the strong women of this country who finally achieved woman suffrage when I was two years old. Yes, I know that was fourteen years after your country had granted women the vote. This is a very big country with much diversity, and therefore some changes come more slowly.

I am haunted by the faces of children who called me teacher thirty and forty years ago. I am haunted by my own children's dreams. I am haunted by memories of myself when I first started school at the age of five and could speak no English, and the teacher and the other students knew that I was stupid.

Most of all, I am haunted by the ghost of the immigrant miners on The Vermilion Range of Minnesota in the early 1900's. My father was an immigrant miner for a short time. We moved elsewhere when I was four, but I continue to be haunted by the knowledge that working conditions in the underground mines in those days were inhuman. Many immigrant miners died. And I continue to be haunted by the knowledge that miners were blacklisted and vilified when they dared to ask for basic safety measures. I am also haunted by the knowledge that my mother almost died at my birth because the doctor at first refused to come because of who we were, and the midwife was helpless because of the difficult delivery. For the rest of her days my mother was terrified of doctors and longed to return home to Finland, a dream never fulfilled.

Which brings me back to you, my Finnish Ghost. I realize now that I would miss you if you left. I love your people, your language, your music, your literature. I love your theater where your people have been able to express the deepest emotions, which their reticence might otherwise stifle. I admire your magnificent contemporary architecture, your beautiful modern designs of fabrics, glassware, and furniture that you have created after the devastation of the Winter War and the Continuation War. I love your land with its lakes and pines and birches, your land, which I have been privileged to visit several times. Most of all, I admire your courage. Please stay with me, my Finnish Ghost. You are a part of me.

The Generations

Do you read those novels about old New England families, generation after generation living and dying in the same house, one of those big white houses with shutters and wraparound verandas where lovers meet? They seldom talk about their roots. They live right in the midst of theirs, with Father and Mother, who are both pillars of society.

I put away the book, page through an old album. See this snapshot? I'd guess around 1938. All immigrants, some by way of Ellis Island. They sip coffee from saucers, Uncle David with a sugar lump poised between his teeth. All the grownups have gathered around Aunt Hilma's big kitchen table for Sunday afternoon coffee.

There's Mama on the left, her dark curly hair swept up in a bun. Aunt Hilma is her sister-in-law. Mama went first, so suddenly. It was September 1955, the year the song "Autumn Leaves" became popular. To this day I can't bear to hear it. Next to her sits Aunt Lydia in her polka dot dress. She is Papa's sister. She left us twenty years later, just as the lilacs bloomed in May. I cried so hard. I cried for her and Mama both. Mama never lived to see her granddaughter.

And there are the three uncles—Uncle Wilho, Uncle Otto, Uncle David—now all gone. Aunt Hilma, the youngest, was the last to leave us. It was in the summer of 1987. I almost forgot that Papa died down in Florida in June 1978, where he had lived the last twenty years. It didn't seem a proper place to die, to be buried without spruces for shade. The sun beats down, dries up the flowers. But that's how his second wife wanted it. She's remarried again. The roses wither. The grass dies.

Our people moved far across oceans, learned foreign ways, a foreign language. Fighting homesickness, they set up new homes, moved again and again to where work could be had. "Where are our roots?" our children ask. Novels don't tell us.

A Different View

September 1986

Youth and age. It's all relative, like the four seasons we adjust to every year The morning's September chill sends me scurrying for a sweater. I trip over cardboard boxes labeled for the movers, trip over remnants of 45 years of marriage, arthritis in my right hip upsetting my balance.

Yesterday the realtor came and nailed a one-word announcement — SOLD — over our "For Sale" sign. I sighed with relief. No more open houses, no more strangers peering into cupboards, closets, checking my housekeeping. Yet I feel an emptiness. A young bride will pick my lilacs in May, open these blinds every morning. Ours will be a different view — from the third floor balcony of our new condominium. Our grown children encourage our move. We know they are right.

We imagine how it will be at first. No more driving up this curving driveway. We will park our car in an underground garage, a garage large enough for over seventy cars. We will smile at unfamiliar faces in the elevators, corridors, mature faces like ours, perhaps exchange names, pleasantries. We will hurry to the security of our own door, #319, hurry to our familiar possessions — the old bookcase, family pictures, the piano.

The collection of labeled boxes grows each day, although we do leave out belongings destined for: (a) The Children, (b) Goodwill, (c) The Garage Sale. Ah, yes, THE GARAGE SALE looms alarmingly between today and MOVING DAY. We calm down a bit when the children assure us they will help. We feel old, older than we are.

I flip through dozens of record albums . Can't part with a single one. I waste half the afternoon listening to old pop tunes, songs of our youth: Moonlight Serenade, Tuxedo Junction, I Know That You Know, These Foolish Things Remind Me of You. Waves of nostalgia wash over me. And then there are Joan Baez, Buffy Sainte-Marie, Pete Seeger, not to mention Janis Ian, Barbara Streisand, Willie Nelson. I throw my hands up in exhaustion and frustration when

I get to the classics. Mozart, Beethoven, and Pavarotti end up on the dining room floor.

I suddenly come to my senses. I don't have to part with any of these: the albums, cassettes, music books, sheet music, stereo, piano. I will make room! I will take them all! My friend Elsie did, and her condo's smaller than ours.

I feel an excitement about the future. I take time out to go to the mail box. The usual junk mail, also Newsweek, and tucked between them an envelope postmarked San Diego. It looks like it might contain a wedding announcement. Could it be? Sure enough, it's from our niece. I laugh with delight as I read:

> *We are happy to announce*
> *our marriage*
> *on Saturday, the fourth of October,*
> *at sunrise.*
> *The wedding will take place in a*
> *hot air balloon over the vineyards*
> *of Temecula, California.*

With new energy I return to packing record albums, pull out several and put them in an empty box that I label:

Music for the Children.

I pull wide the bay window drapes to let the sun in, watch a flock of blackbirds gathering on the lawn, preparing for their autumn flight south. They know it is time.

Hotel Villas Telemar

Honduras
February 1980

Laughing excitedly like children, we inspect our newly-rented villa facing the Caribbean, the beach as lovely as the brochure claims:

> **LUXURIOUS VILLAS: The City of Tela, famous all over America for its beautiful beaches, is now even more exciting with the new Hotel Villas Telamar**

We are three middle-aged couples from Minnesota who have come to Honduras, to its port city of Tela, to escape winter, to soak up the sun, to swim, sail, scuba dive, and to try out our high school Spanish.

We race down to the beach to test the water, the hot sun burning our feet. A ship appears on the horizon, between us a sea of tranquil amethyst. Not a ripple, not a wave. Nearby, vultures comb the beach. A strange bird cries in a eucalyptus tree. Within sight, a long pier with railroad tracks juts out to sea, beside it a big freighter.

The next morning we are all awakened abruptly at 4 A.M. A huge blast of sound shakes our villa. It sounds twice more at half hour intervals. Dogs begin barking outside and roosters crow. It is absolutely impossible to sleep late at Telamar. Our protests are futile. The big sound cannot be silenced, we are told. It is the morning call to Tela's banana workers, time to get the lead out, time to load bananas on the freighter, out to world markets. We learn that the fifty villas in our fenced-in compound, Hotel Villas Telamar, are the former residences of United Fruit Company executives. We are now in the Banana Republic of Honduras where not one banana can be purchased at the market.

One day we drive into the country in a rented van, six Americans viewing local color in air-conditioned comfort. An old crippled man trudges toward us, a huge load of kindling on his back. High on the mountainside, field hands work in the hot sun. A group of young children walk in pairs along the dusty roadside, seven and eight-year old little girls carrying their younger brothers and sisters in their arms, learning at a tender age what a mother has to do.

One of our group, who is driving our van, suddenly stops and steps out of the van to take pictures in front of a small cottage. I thought it to be an uninvited intrusion when suddenly a young girl runs hurriedly into the front yard, picks up her baby sister and, with hostile backward glances toward us, runs behind white sheets drying on the line and escapes our brazen camera. We are the "Ugly Americans." I blush with shame.

Hi-Jacked In Stockholm

It was the summer of 1983. My husband and I were planning a trip to Finland, when we learned that a Norwegian-American group in Minnesota had extra round-trip travel tickets to Stockholm that were selling at a low price. We hurried to buy the tickets and felt very lucky to get them, since our scheduled trip would be the last of the season. With four weeks allowed between arrival in Stockholm and returning home, those four weeks would give us time to take the Silja Line for a cruise from Stockholm to Finland, as well as time to visit a number of relatives in Helsinki and time to return to Stockholm.

We arrived at the Hubert H. Humphrey Charter Terminal early on the given day of departure, all packed up and eager to get going. Neither my husband nor I had ever been at this Terminal, since our previous travels out of the United States had always started from the main Minneapolis Airport. We began to feel a bit uneasy, although neither one of us said so out loud. But I did say to myself: "If this is good enough for the Norwegian-Americans, it should be good enough for us." There was a long waiting period before we could check in our luggage. By the time we entered the plane, I was so tired I barely noticed how small it was, and how dingy it looked.

We found seats near the front of the plane. Across the aisle was the kitchen, where two young flight-attendants had to rush around with little time to rest, or they would be reprimanded by their manager. Much of the flight was at night. After a late dinner, as I recall, I slept most of the night. In the morning we were served breakfast, and we all began to be excited as we were approaching Oslo, Norway, for a short stop on our way to Stockholm. Many of our Norwegian-American travelers got off in Oslo. But the rest of us continued our flight to Stockholm, with several still left in the plane. As we flew over the fjords in Norway, the view was breathtaking.

When we finally arrived at the airport in Stockholm around noon, the passengers scattered hither and yon. We soon got a taxi that took us to the center of Stockholm, which we planned to explore, since neither one of us had been in Stockholm before. But we were out of luck. The temperature in Stockholm was unusually hot that week. You could hardly see anyone walking on the streets. We managed to find the Jarlsborg Hotel, where we had lunch that day, and where we were lucky enough to get a room for the last days of our stay before going back to Minnesota. Those days turned out to be so good that we wished we could stay longer.

Then finally came the day when it was time to go home. We hired a Stockholm taxi to take us to the airport. Our cab driver was delightful. He laughed and smiled all the way, talking in Swedish and we in English. We managed best with gestures. When we arrived at the airport, our cab driver insisted on carrying every piece of our luggage into the airport all by himself. How could things be better, I thought, with everything working out so smoothly!

Little did we know. We felt very organized, with our luggage checked in already, and with plenty of time to eat a delicious luncheon that was served to us at the airport. And now it was time to change our money from Swedish Krona to American money. Next we were led, together with many other travelers, into a huge room with chairs and small tables, and a large window facing the airport where a plane sat on the tarmac. Perhaps it is the plane that will soon fly us home to Minnesota, I thought. It was 12:00 noon, and we were scheduled to leave at 1:00 p.m. We spent that hour getting to meet our fellow travelers, all headed for Minneapolis, a few of whom we knew and others that we were meeting for the first time. Our group consisted of over one hundred adults, and a few children.

We were all excited, but many wondered why only one plane sat in view and there were no sounds of planes going up or coming down, and the clock already said 2:30 p.m. Some of us inquired what was going on. The staff was gracious but only mumbled something about a short delay.

Some of us began to get edgy, and since we got no clear explanation from the captain and staff, we were getting angry. We realized that the plane on the tarmac was the only one we had seen all this time even though the staff said the runway is too busy now. One of the women in our group was so frustrated that she screamed and went up to the captain, grabbed him by his shoulders and shook him so hard that his cap fell off. Then the children started crying, they were so frightened.

Many of us started worrying about our families back home. We were given permission to phone them but were told that we couldn't be called back. I did phone home and covered up what was happening. I just said that we were fine but we would be arriving home later than initially planned. We noticed that everyone's luggage had been brought out and piled high on a platform outside. We weren't allowed to get them.

The clock now said five o'clock in the afternoon, and the captain and his staff continued to avoid us. We all began to have differing ideas about what was happening. But nobody was sure. It was scary. But now our concern began to center on food. Everyone was hungry. Finally we complained so loud that the staff brought us some canned goods and crackers from the plane. We were told sharply not to try to go to the plane.

At one point, between six and seven o'clock, when most of us were exhausted and frightened, we noticed a group of about ten men and women entering the room, all attired in police garb. They lined up stiffly in a row, all facing us, but saying nothing. For a moment I thought they had come to rescue us. But then I realized that they were here to make sure none of us tried to go to the plane.

The mystery of this whole episode finally, slowly, unraveled itself late in the evening, starting around 10 p.m.

None of us had known that a very rich business man from Stockholm was deeply involved. He was the whole key to this mystery. We also learned that he had been on the flight from Oslo to Stockholm when we were on it. And we learned that the Travel Agency that chartered this particular flight was operated out of Kansas. It was the rich business man who had loaned the money for the Norwegian-American summer flights to Norway, and the Travel Agency was very late in its payments.

So what happened next was telephone call after telephone call from the Stockholm Airport to the Travel Agency in Kansas. Since it was late in the evening in Stockholm and early in the morning in Kansas, nobody could be reached by phone at first. But finally a call went through, and the rich business man from Stockholm got what Kansas owed him — something like $85,000 dollars we were told.

We were very tired travelers when we were finally allowed to leave for home. We boarded our flight at 11:00 p.m. Within a few minutes we were all served a good dinner. It was the last flight of the season, and therefore the plane was over-loaded, but we managed somehow to squeeze into our seats. We were flown home by the way of the Baffin Islands, where we stopped briefly for fuel, and then continued our flight, eager to get home. We arrived at the Minneapolis airport at 6:30 in the morning.

We all had an unexpected surprise when we got our luggage. A smelly fish oil had been spilled, deliberately I'm sure, on everyone's luggage, including my new suitcase which had just been given to me by my husband as a birthday gift. We never did find out who the culprit was. The rich business man from Stockholm never showed up. It was just as well. What was important was that we all arrived home safely.

To Grandmother's House

      Multia, Finland   September, 1984

We are of the same generation, Hilja and I,
she a grandmother, widow of my cousin,
mistress of this big house.
I am the American guest in her home.

The old Finnish farmhouse sits high on a hill
as it has since the 1600's,
nine generations of the Ylätalo family.
The maples are ablaze with September colors.
The potato crop has just been dug.
It could be Indian Summer in Minnesota.

I study Grandmother Kristiina's portrait on the wall.
I never knew her — just a small, dim picture
that Mother brought to America in 1913.
Mother rarely talked about her. It was too painful.
Hilja points out the pictures of Grandmother's sisters —
Erika, Johanna, Maria. Kristiina was the prettiest,
Hilja says, as though to please me.
It is all so strange, so long ago.

I feel a chill. Hilja urges me to rest, brings me a blanket.
I lie down on the couch, begin to feel young, protected.
Hilja grows older as I listen to her bustling sounds
in the kitchen. She is becoming my mother.

We have a light supper,
for dessert a warm rice pudding full of plump raisins.
We talk late into the night. Hilja says, yes, she understands
my Finnish. She laughs a lot, her cheeks rosy like Mother's,
her eyes a crystal blue.
She promises to reheat the rice pudding for breakfast.
I keep growing younger.

In the morning Hilja wakes me up gently.
She is my grandmother.
It is my first visit to my grandmother's house.

Off To Bayhead We Go

It was the summer of 1941. I had just arrived in Washington, D.C. from Minnesota. The train trip had been exhausting, but I forgot about it because I was so happy knowing that in a few minutes I would join my fiance, Oliver, who had come to Washington, D.C. a year ago. I had stayed in Minnesota that year since I had already signed a year's contract to teach high school classes in a southern Minnesota town. Oliver and I had graduated from the University of Minnesota, where we met, the same year, 1940. The decision was made early in the spring of 1941 that I would cancel my contract at the school for the following year and join Oliver in Washington, D.C., where he already had a job with the Justice Department, and where I would have time that summer to find a job. Fortunately I did find a job as a secretary with the Board of Governors of the Federal Reserve system a few weeks after I arrived.

The train terminal was packed with travelers. It seemed like forever, but finally we saw each other in the crowd, and what a terrific meeting it was. The past year had seemed like a century.

A few weeks after my arrival, Oliver's sister, Ella, who lived in New Jersey, invited us to Bayhead, New Jersey, an ocean side summer place where she worked for a wealthy family. We were quite excited and took a train, as people usually traveled in those days. It was a delightful time, swimming in the ocean and resting on the beach. We met some of the members of the wealthy family, who treated us with esteem when

Oliver and I near the ocean at Bayhead, New Jersey.

they discovered that we were University graduates! I can still remember the delicious meals that Ella made for us.

That summer will always be very special for me, beginning with our trip to Bayhead a few weeks before we were married in September. Ella was my maid of honor.

There were rumors of war, of Hitler, a name foreign to us then. We put it aside. We were so happy in our own "safe" little world, which lasted until the fall of 1942. Like thousands of other young American men, my young husband was drafted to serve in World War II over seas.

I returned to Minnesota, where I found work in an office in Minneapolis for the War Manpower Commission. It was a good job, but every day I read the newspapers for news about how the war is going. Every day, for three years, I screened the papers. And finally it came, The war had ended! Columbus Day, 1945.

We were finally able to have a real family, a real home, which we did. But the years have gone by fast, and our three children are grown up, with their own homes now, as it should be. Sometimes I find myself reminiscing about the days at Bayhead and in Washington D.C. when I was so young and my whole life still ahead of me. Great memories!

Oliver and I in Washington, D.C.

Our Trip Out West

It was early June in 1964 when our family made a decision to visit Aunt Pearl and her family in Montana that summer. Our family consisted of Father, Mother, three children (ages 4, 12, and 16), and our cocker spaniel named Penny. Diane was the youngest, Alan the twelve-year old, and Bob the oldest. It would be our first trip to the far west and to visit Aunt Pearl's family.

After some discussion, we agreed to lengthen our trip by going first through South Dakota so we could see the Black Hills and Mt. Rushmore, then to Yellowstone, and finally to Glacier National Park in Montana, which was not far from Aunt Pearl's home in Valier, Montana. We had learned that Aunt Pearl and

Oliver, Alan, I, Diane, Pearl, Mark. Mr. Stoltz and our dog Penny.

her husband, Charles, had a big ranch near Valier and oil wells on their land — and horses! Our boys were as excited about that as was my husband, Oliver.

It was a calm, sunny summer day in the Twin Cities when we began our trip in our Rambler Station Wagon, to which my husband had attached a Teepee trailer. He was an outdoors man and a wildlife biologist, so he knew how to plan for wilderness trips. We felt well prepared for our trip — food, clothing, blankets, sleeping bags, flashlights, maps, etc.

The drive to the South Dakota border went relatively well. Only once did we miss the right turn on the road when we approached the border. Once past it, we began to look for picnic grounds where we could stop over night. We finally spotted one that advertised a lake by it, .so we drove in. Then we saw that the lake had dried out. What a disappointment for the children. It was already getting]ate in the afternoon. We had no choice but to park there. We spread out our sandwiches, fruit, and milk containers on a picnic table, when car after car drove in and then drove out, their occupants staring at us as though we had just arrived from Mars. Finally the parade ended and the local folks disappeared.

The sun was beginning to set, so we arranged sleeping conditions for the night — Oliver, Diane and me in the Teepee trailer and the boys in the station wagon. The next morning we woke up to another sunny day. Everyone had slept well, including Penny. We had a quick breakfast, eager to get on the road.

I had arranged a space in the back of the Station Wagon, where Penny could

Picnic on our trip out West.

lie down on a blanket. But she preferred to come up closer to the rest of us, and she would wrap her furry body around my neck. I endured it at first, but when the day began to get warmer and warmer (no air conditioning back then) I had to place Penny back on her blanket.

The drive went along smoothly for a while, but then we all began to suffer from the heat. It must have been over a hundred degrees. We finally got to Wahl's Drugstore, which was on our way. We stopped there to cool off a bit and to buy some cards and presents for folks back home .

Then we continued our trip, now eagerly waiting to get to Rapid City, which is at the base of the Black Hills. What a blessing the Black Hills were. As we drove higher and higher, it got cooler and cooler . Just what we wanted. Then Mt. Rushmore appeared, so close and so awesome. We spent the night in the Black Hills. The following day our trip through Wyoming was long and tiring. We went up high in the Bighorn Mountains where we spent the night .

The next day again required a lot of driving as we headed toward Yellowstone National Park. Eventually we got there to the excitement of all of us, especially our finally seeing the Old Faithful Geyser go up. Oliver, Penny and the two boys stayed over night in the station wagon and our Teepee trailer. I rented a motel room for Diane and me because we were getting jittery after having heard bears the night before on the Bighorn Mountain. So we insisted on a motel room.

The next day we began our final trip, which was to Montana's beautiful

Alan fishing In Montana's Glacier National Park.

Glacier National Park, as well as our special visit to the Stoltz family in Valier, Montana. Words can't express what a delightful several days we had with the Stoltzes.

We all learned a great deal on our trip, especially discovering that there is nothing to compare with what nature has created.

We returned to Minnesota by way of North Dakota, happy with our trip, yet also anxious to get home.

Old Faithful.

Our family at Old Faithful.

Fiction:

The Middle Years

It was 3 p.m. and Ruth was angry. She swished the brandy in her glass with such fury that it spilled over the edge, dribbled down her fingers onto the collar of her new pretty blue dress. But she didn't notice. There were so many things to be angry about. Underneath the anger was an overwhelming sadness that she didn't dare to look at. And so she concentrated on being angry, about being alone, about what had happened at lunch.

Ruth stared out of an eighth floor window of the Mayflower Hotel, the Washington, D.C. home of senators and ex-presidents, the Mayflower Hotel where the dining room menu still bragged that J. Edgar Hoover still had a permanently reserved table for his daily lunch there. Ruth stared out at the third day of unrelenting rain, at the continued heaviness of the late September sky. It had rained non-stop since their jet arrived from Minneapolis Tuesday evening.

Where was John? He had said that the conference would break up early this afternoon. The rest of today and tonight was all that was left for them, all that was left of their 35th wedding anniversary. She had had so many plans.

A fine way to spend a second honeymoon, she thought. Here they were in Washington, D.C. where they were married in October 1945 but where nothing was the same. Ruth returned to the window to stare at the rain and at her only view, the dreary activities in the dreary law office across the way. There were no shining views of the White House or the Capitol or the Lincoln Memorial, but a much too clear a view of the pompous executive who sat swiveling in his chair, mouthing insinuations to a young woman, long-lashed and slender-waisted, and shouting orders to a shapeless, middle-aged woman who was obviously the work horse of the office. It added fuel to Ruth's anger because she had been just like that woman for two years. That is, until two and a half years ago, when she walked out without giving a minute's notice.

Still no John. She thought how different he was from the attorney across the way, and her anger began to melt. John was as quiet-spoken and unassuming when they had lunch today in the hotel coffee shop as when they first met in college 37 years ago. He had been so handsome then, tall, slender and dark-haired. Now at 58, he was almost as handsome. His hair had grayed and his face had matured in gentle lines. Only his eyes held a new tension and sadness, and he sighed with a weariness that Ruth tried to ignore as they studied their luncheon menus.

"Cocktail?" John asked. As always, he was a man of few words. Not so Ruth. Not anymore. But when they were first married she was shy and quiet. Too long ago for John to remember.

"You know they only serve drinks in the dining room," Ruth said. She knew she sounded irritated and knew she was treading on dangerous ground. But it was almost as if an inner force was compelling her to continue to be ugly.

"Why didn't we go to the dining room? You know this is our last day. You could have made reservations."

Bob chose not to answer. They sat in silence until the waiter came. Then they both ordered salads and drank their coffee without a word. John seemed far away, and Ruth didn't like his preoccupation. She was sure it had nothing to do with the conference, or he would have shared it with her. It was only personal agonies he had difficulty voicing. Even to her, after all these years. Even if they were also her agonies.

But she had to know about tonight. Where they would be going. He hadn't given her even a hint. She wanted to know what time she should be ready. And it was important for her to know that he had made the plans, that he had wanted to make the plans. At this moment it was more important to her than anything else in the world. There was still time to recapture what was drifting away so fast. She had to have this memory. She had to have it. It would help ease some of the pain of the past five years. She knew it would. For both of them. It had to.

Finally she spoke. She succeeded in keeping her voice quiet, but the questions came tumbling out in almost one breath.

"John, where will we be going tonight? Will the long, pink dress I brought along be all right, do you think? What time should we get started?"

The salads arrived but neither of them noticed.

"What would you like to do?" he asked.

"What do you mean, 'What would I like to do?'"

John was startled by the sharpness of her question.

"You mean you haven't made reservations any place for tonight?

You know it's too late to get tickets anymore." She didn't know that for sure. That's now what she was angry about, and she was not going to admit why she was. But Ruth suddenly realized that her voice was getting loud, and she lowered her eyes to avoid nearby stares.

Quiet John exploded. "You know I haven't had time to do anything like that this week. I've been busy with meetings. Why didn't you make reservations or get tickets if that's what you wanted. You had plenty of time. I've hardly looked at the papers, so I don't know what's going on."

"You have read the papers every evening." Ruth's voice was low, but she enunciated every syllable with exaggerated clarity. "You've read every editorial. You know you have. And you knew that I wanted to go to the Kennedy Center." She stood up and added, "Some second honeymoon," and then walked out of the coffee shop without looking back, left John with two untouched salads and undoubtedly many curious stares, knew his embarrassment and didn't care a fig.

Ruth was dry-eyed, but she shook with anger as she walked through the crowded lobby toward the elevators. She was furious all the way to the eighth floor, through the long walk through winding corridors to their room. She fumbled with her key, finally got the door open, slammed it shut, kicked off her shoes as far as she could kick, shouted "Damn! Damn! Damn!", threw her purse across the room, and slumped into the only comfortable chair in the small $58.00 a day room. She sat in a silent knot of anger for ten minutes, then heaved a big sigh, got up, and still dry-eyed, poured herself a stiff drink of brandy at exactly 1 p.m.

Until two years ago, Ruth rarely drank except on special social occasions, nor did John. But she knew he had started drinking secretly, and sometimes heavily, two years ago. She found hidden bottles, empty and half empty, in the strangest places. He was clever, but not clever enough for her. She wondered if he knew that she also started drinking alone soon after he did. She helped empty his half-empty bottles, very carefully concealing them again exactly where she had found them. About a year ago was the first time in her life that she entered a liquor store alone and purchased her first bottle of hard liquor. She had made several purchases since.

However, after starting to see Ann, a Gestalt therapist, last June, Ruth knew she had gradually made progress, felt better about herself, and had cut her drinking to an occasional highball before dinner. No hidden drinking.

Her progress was clearly helping John, but when she suggested that he could personally benefit from similar therapy he blew up and she never dared mention it again. But this afternoon her vow not to drink alone was forgotten.

Ruth returned to the window and saw the young secretary with the slender waist lean over the desk and smile into the eyes of the man old enough to be her father. "I had a figure like that once," Ruth thought. In fact John would have told her that it was better than that even when she was forty, a year before her third and last child was born.

She walked back toward the mirror above the low chest, backed away toward the opposite wall so she could study her full length. With the long loose top of her new dress, her thickening waistline was camouflaged, and she looked taller and more slender than she really was. The color of her dress complemented the dark of her hair, now starting to frost with gray around her face. Her eyes were still large and of the brightest blue. But there were new lines beginning to pull down the corners of her mouth. The baby face of her youth, which always made people think she was several years younger than she really was, was starting to droop and sag into a grandmotherly look.

And that is what she was, a grandmother and also full-time mother to her only grandchild, three-year old Billy. His mother, their beautiful daughter Jill, their first born, had died in a car crash two years ago. Jill's husband had left her months before the baby was born. No one knew where he was, or cared. Jill would have been thirty last month.

Is that when it all started, when their cozy world began to crumble? Was that the dividing line? Even with the brandy she was still trying not to look further back.

"Don't forget your breakdown!" The words seemed to jump at her from somewhere inside her.

Five years ago. Was it that long ago? The years fly by so fast. So many things had happened just before that. Illnesses and deaths came in triplicate. A wrong medical diagnosis of their son Mark, then ten, and ensuing complications sent them to the Mayo Clinic after two years of bewilderment and fright. There they straightened everything out very neatly except for Mark's recurring fear and distrust of doctors. A month later Ruth folded up like a broken sparrow for six months.

But John carried on stoically through it all because that is what men are supposed to do. She was glad that he knew how to cry. Sometimes Ruth would find him crying quietly in a far-off corner of the house, and she knew he needed to be alone.

"Ruth, there is still a full life for you," Ann told her in July. "For you, your husband, your family." Ruth liked Ann, liked her warmth, liked her when she scolded her. Their ages were similar and somehow she felt Ann knew so much because of what she herself had lived through, not just because of her professional training. It had been so different with the male Freudian shrink who had further messed up her mind and spirit five years ago. He would write on his yellow pad when she felt she was saying nothing significant and yawned in her face when she was spilling her guts. Ann had never written down one word during a session.

And so they had planned this trip. John was already scheduled to go to Washington in late October for an educational conference. And it seemed so right because the place and time of year were significant to them. Billy was Ruth's biggest concern. Billy was Ruth's biggest concern. But Amy, their quiet daughter, now 22, and so like John, insisted on spending her vacation taking care of Billy. And Mark, now 15, was like a brother to Billy.

Ruth had had no lunch. The third brandy was making her nauseated. The only food in the room, a small handful of peanuts, was consumed after her first drink. It was now 4:30, and still no John. She began to cry. She didn't blame him if he didn't come back. He was too patient with her, too long-suffering. She wasn't making any sense. Of course he would come back. All his luggage was here.

The thought cheered her up, and she checked her wardrobe for what she would wear for the morning flight home. Then she hesitated as she looked at the long green and gold gown and the matching gold fringed shawl. Maybe there was still a chance that they could at least go downstairs for dinner.

She heard the knock at the door and hurried to open it. John stood there, his dark blue suit soaked, his gray hair plastered in wet strands to his head. His expression terrified her.

Ruth turned away and sat down in the chair. Without a word he went into the bathroom and took a long shower, the longest shower he had probably ever taken. He changed into fresh dry clothes. Not one word was said.

He poured himself a drink. And then he started. Never in all their married years had he said as much to her in a whole month as he shouted at her in the next several minutes. Ruth didn't listen much to what he said, mostly to how he said it. Her head was down so she couldn't see his face, but she was sure it must be as dark as midnight.

Did she know that he had not attended the conference after lunch? He emphasized the word "lunch." Not even one minute of it, even though it was the most important session of the conference? And she knew darn well why he didn't. Did she know that he had been walking the streets of Washington D.C. for hours in the rain, and that he didn't give a damn about Kennedy Centers or party gowns or second honeymoons and that he was sick of her darn carping and that he was going out to get drunk.

All of the eighth floor must have heard his announcement, and when he slammed the door on departing, there was no question that he meant what he said.

Ruth sat in the chair a long time. She was no longer nauseated. And surprisingly, she didn't feel as bad about John's outburst as she thought she should. Maybe this purging of his gut feelings was a good sign. Yes, that was it. He was alive again. Certainly he had a mountain of rage and sadness stored up inside, long overdue to come out. And suddenly she was sure his uncharacteristic threat to go out and get drunk was not to be taken seriously.

But an hour went by, and he hadn't returned. The phone rang, and Ruth stumbled as she ran to answer. But it was Amy calling from home.

"Something wrong, Mom? Your voice sounds funny."

"Oh, I picked up a bit of a cold. All it does here is rain."

"Well, happy anniversary, Mom. We all send our love. Is Dad there?"

"Sorry. He—he stepped out. I—I think to get some wine," Ruth half-lied. "How's everything? she added.

"Just great. And we'll be at the airport tomorrow. Billy says hi. Bye," Mom."

Ruth put down the receiver and began to sob. Huge sobs enveloped her whole body. She throbbed with the agonies of the past five years. Finally she quieted and lay exhausted on the bed.

She didn't know what time it was when there was a soft knock at the door. But she heard it and knew it was John. Slowly, quietly, with dried tears streaking her face, her hair disheveled, she got up and went to the door. Calmly she opened it.

They held each other for a long time.

Avery Hall
(Fiction)

The letter arrived in the middle of June. The envelope was so small it looked like it might be one of those bridal shower invitations. The handwriting was dainty and precise. Vaguely familiar. But there was no return address. I groaned as I started opening it. I just couldn't cope with another bridal shower. There had been three already in the past few weeks, and the thought of another afternoon of parlor games and prizes and oohing over one more set of pink bath towels was more than I could bear.

It turned out to be a letter from Sally, my college roommate. That in itself was a surprise since, while we still kept in touch after 36 years, it narrowed down long ago to Christmas notes and cards. And we have seen each other only two times since we graduated in 1942. The last time was ten years ago when we happened to meet at a teachers' conference. Sally looked great then, and her long blond hair was as beautiful as ever.

The letter was short, but the first few lines threw me off balance for a few minutes. Then I consulted my calendar and found I was free for lunch on Saturday, July 10. I had no previous commitments unless I decided to make one up. And don't think I wasn't tempted.

I reread the note. Sally started out with her familiar goody-two-shoes routine: "Our dreams have finally come true. We will definitely have a reunion of the third floor girls of Avery Hall. As you remember, Ann, I mentioned this possibility in my Christmas note."

Actually, I didn't remember any such thing, nor did I remember ever having had such a dream. But then I thought to myself, "I'm getting old and grouchy. Where's my old school spirit?" After some thought I remembered how much I had looked forward to seeing Sally the first time after we graduated. But we were young then, and a lot of things were happening, exciting things, and we both expected the future would bring with it so much more. It's a good thing none of us know what's around each of those bends ahead.

I went back to reading the letter: "Mary Olson and I have been planning this since last summer," Sally wrote," and it seems that almost everybody whom we have contacted from out of town can come, Joyce from Washington, D.C., Lois from Michigan, Jane from Iowa, Marge from Hazelville, and Laura, who still lives in Minneapolis and can definitely make it. Ann, we do hope you can come. We don't have Laura's and Edna's addresses, so please contact them and then phone Mary, since she is making the reservations." The remainder of the letter gushed about how wonderful it would be, and Sally added parenthetically that she and her husband, Dave, were still unpacking after having recently moved into a year-round lake home about seventy miles from Minneapolis. I was surprised that they could retire so early, but perhaps because Dave was several years older than Sally. I really didn't know much about him. It all sounded so ideal, and I felt that old twinge of envy.

I had no idea who Jane from Iowa was, or some of the other names she mentioned, but then, Sally had lived at Avery Hall for longer than I. But something in the back of my mind triggered off a memory: the name Mary Olson. I spent the next hour looking for an old snapshot, and at last I found it. There we were, the four of us, lined up posing in our caps and gowns on the lawn on the west side of the dorm: Sally, Jenny, Mary, and me. Sally was poised and beautiful, with her sweet twist of a smile that made the fellows swoon; Jenny was overweight and with that perennially sleepy expression; Mary was poised and serious and overweight; as for me, I looked all of fifteen and still shy. I couldn't have weighed more than 95 pounds. Obviously the college years hadn't added an ounce of weight, or poise.

Still only half-decided, I tried to phone Mary, but her line was busy. I remembered seeing Mary once after graduation. It was about 1950 when a number of us met Sally for lunch when she was in between buses on her way home for Christmas. She was an only child, and her parents lived in a small town in Illinois. That was when Sally was teaching in a college in the South. We were all so excited about Sally's engagement to a professor. But then we always knew she would go far. Most of the rest of us had already been married for several years except for those who never did get married. And Mary Olson, who I would have predicted would be a career woman, had taught English for only one year and then settled down happily as a wife and a mother of two children.

I dialed Mary again and reached her. I wondered whether Mary would remember me. But right away it was as though we had just seen each other last week. She sounded happy and content in a mature, matter-of-fact way. Well, she had been mature and matter-of-fact 36 years ago. "Ann, I'm still overweight," she said easily, with a laugh in her voice. "I sure hope you can come," she added. To my own surprise, I promised to come without hesitation. I said that I couldn't contact Vivien. Mary said that Vivien had died two years ago. We both remembered her and felt sad. She had been the free spirit among our group and had lived it to the fullest, including her last year, when she knew she was dying.

Having had the pep talk from Mary, I put in a call to Edna. "You've got to be kidding," was her quick reply. "Do you have a conflict?" I asked, unwilling to give up so fast, knowing I had to pursue it carefully with Edna. "I'm sure I can think of one," was Edna's quick response. "Oh, come on," I said. "It wouldn't be so bad. And I'd feel so much more comfortable if you came. Why don't you and Eric come down for the whole weekend. Paul and Eric could go fishing or play golf that day, and in the evening we could go to the Guthrie, or whatever you like. How about it?"

"Why would I want to have lunch with a bunch of women whom I haven't seen since 1939?" Edna said. "Well you've seen me," I said. "You know what I mean," was her answer. "What about Mary? She said you two couples were in a square dance group together back in the '50's, when her husband and Eric were completing their Ph.Ds. And she said her husband still sees Eric at meetings."

"I don't remember her at all," Edna said. "Honest. And I really do have other plans for that day. I'm sorry, Ann. Really I am." Edna's voice had softened, but she didn't relent, and my old feelings of inferiority began to build as I hung up the phone and thought of facing that group alone.

My husband, Paul, encouraged me to go. "You'll enjoy seeing Sally again. She sure was a cute spitfire with that long blond hair and big blue eyes." Suddenly I felt jealous. I was surprised that the old jealousy was still there. How stupid.

It hadn't been easy being Sally's roommate. She was the most popular girl on the third floor, if not the entire dorm. Certainly the prettiest. And smart too, as well as the favorite of the House Mother. The House Mother was an elegant silver-haired dorm director, who would handpick her special girls to dine with her at her round table seating four. Sally was often among the chosen, and she had all the social skills to feel comfortable dining with her. In fact, she carried it off with a flair that almost bordered on arrogance. I, on the other hand, would have been tongue-tied and miserable. But then there was never any danger of my being so honored.

I first met Sally when I transferred to Avery Hall from another college. She had a double room across the hall from Edna and me. Sally's roommate was Jean, a thin brown wren of a girl. Jean spoke rarely and then almost inaudibly, and seemed to meld unnoticed into the woodwork when their room was crowded with Sally's friends. But I also remembered that there was more to Jean than was outwardly apparent—in fact there were rumors then that she was a mathematical genius. Jean and Edna both graduated when Sally and I were still juniors, and that is how I became Sally's roommate in my last year. And suddenly I became interested in seeing Jean again and wondered what all these years had done to her.

July 1976 was very hot, and the day of July 10 was the hottest. The air conditioning in the house went out during the night, and my hair was limp ten minutes after I had removed the rollers and sprayed it with super strength hair spray. My favorite blue dress, which was so flattering last summer, was too tight around the middle. I had lost five pounds since the invitation arrived, but I had gained over ten in the past year, and all the extra pounds we all concentrated at the waistline. Frustrated, I finally chose a cool green and white pants suit and wondered why I cared so much about how I looked. But I fretted all the way downtown, positive that everyone else would be wearing a dress. I tried to push away the feelings of inadequacy, just like when I'd travel to visit my 85-year-old father in Florida and, in spite of all my efforts, I'd be transformed into a little girl again.

But I was also beginning to get excited about seeing Sally again. Old memories kept nudging me, some bittersweet, but mostly the good times we had together in our senior year, the only college year I didn't have to work part time. In the fall quarter I met Paul at a twilight dance at the Old Union on campus. Sally was engaged to Jim then, a handsome pre-med from Chicago.

We would double-date and went to many formals together. Those were the days of formal dances when we would wear long gowns and full-length velvet capes. I can still smell the penetrating pungency of the gardenia corsages Paul would send me. And never will I forget Sally in her violet taffeta off-the-shoulder formal and her orchid corsage. Scarlet O'Hara would have scratched her eyes out. But then Sally and Jim broke up, and she refused to talk about it. But I knew that nothing would stop Sally from getting whatever she wanted out of life because Sally had faith and brains and a beautiful soul, and nobody, nobody could say no to those blue eyes and peach blossom skin and that gorgeous long blond hair.

I walked into the lobby of the restaurant where we were to meat ten minutes early, and spied three matronly women and one willowy beautiful creature seated over to the right, two of them staring at me, and all wearing dresses. One of them called out, "Ann how nice." Self-consciously I walked toward the owner of the authoritative but friendly voice. She was plump and gray-haired.

"Mary?" I asked hesitantly as I extended my hand in greeting. Mary squeezed it and smiled with a warmth that made me feel much better. She introduced me to Jane from Iowa, who, I learned was Dr. Jensen, a professor of biology. She was very prim and spoke softly and seemed to have difficulty smiling.

The third woman of the plump trio was Vivien. I had no uncertainty about that. Vivien was still as wide and tall as she was 36 years ago. Her eyelids were drooped in their familiar heavy-lidded position.

They gave her the appearance of being eternally bored. She had nothing to say and said it constantly in a booming, strident monotone. She was unmarried and apparently was still living the same solitary lazy life, the same pattern of 36 years ago when she managed to barely squeak through the graduation. Most of her college days had been spent trying to exert the least amount of effort, particularly physical. Her only passions then were chocolates, solitaire and cheap novels, and probably still are. I pondered about her life now, when the beautiful willowy creature spoke to me. Up until then I was sure she had somehow just happened to be sitting near the other three. But she said my name:

"Ann, I'm so glad to see you after all these years." Her voice was rich and warm and as lovely as her face. Her gray-tinged hair softly framed a face that was as elegantly lean and sculptured as a model's. I was beginning to feel panicky as I tried to place her. Suddenly I was overwhelmed by the realization that she was Jean. Jean, Sally's first roommate, the quiet wraith of a girl who would silently glide by in the hallway with a shy little smile and nod a greeting if you condescended to glance in her direction. Mary whispered to me that Jean was Dr. Smith, that she had taught for years at the University Medical School before leaving for Washington, where she had held a prominent position with HEW for almost 15 years. She was happily not married.

Three more ex-Avery Hall girls arrived, one of them wearing a pants suit. Immediately I felt more comfortable. I recognized Marge instantly. She had hardly changed at all. The other two I didn't know.

Then began the wait for the final guest. Sally still hadn't arrived. And Sally was never late. So against her principles. She had many high principles, and I was sure she never wavered, never compromised.

"Her bus must be late," Mary said. "I know she'll be here." She explained that Sally was afraid to drive into the city and was taking a bus from up north. I couldn't remember Sally ever being afraid of anything.

Just then the varied conversations faded as all eyes gradually turned and riveted toward the door. Everyone called out her name. Yes, it was Sally. The old excitement. The old charm. Unmistakably her walk, and wearing her favorite, most becoming color — a soft peach. And the same twist of a smile. But as she drew nearer, I noticed her familiar determined stride was more of a heavy plop, plop, as though her shoes were made of unbending iron. Then I saw that she was wearing the most unbecoming Red Cross shoes with laces. Incredible to see Sally with old ladies' shoes. And her dress, obviously of the most expensive fabric, was cut in loose, unbecoming lines that added years to her mature figure. Not plump, but mature.

And the peach blossom complexion, her beautiful complexion, had dried and wrinkled, and the sweet crooked smile had settled into a permanent thin-lipped diagonal line when she stopped smiling. But then she smiled again and greeted everyone individually with such warmth, she almost seemed like the Sally I used to know.

Soon we were all seated at a rectangular table in a private room which Mary had reserved, and everyone was ordering food and drinks and chattering away as though 36 years had never been.

I found myself seated between Marge and Jean. Across from me was someone named Gladys whom I didn't know but who I found comfortable and easy to talk to. Sally sat next to her and seemed uncharacteristically subdued, and it distressed me more than I cared to acknowledge. But then I turned to Marge when Jean started talking with Sally. Marge was delightfully candid and cheerful, said she had seven children and six grandchildren. She lived in Hazelville, which she claimed with pride was a hick town of 359 people. And loved it. One of her sons was a priest, another was in medical school, and the two youngest, both girls, were still in college. All I could see were dollar signs and wondered silently how she could be so calm and content with such a heavy financial burden. She said that her children and grandchildren kept her young and aware, and I believed her with all my heart.

I was happy not to be seated next to Vivien, who insisted on shouting every comment and smoking non-stop, her cigarette dramatically held in a long cigarette holder as she surveyed the length of the table with her bored look. I was sorry to see that Mary and somebody named Bernice were stuck with her. But they seemed to be able to hold their own.

I noticed that Sally had ordered a dquirri. Somehow I knew she would because she always did years ago, and I had begun to realize that the clock had stopped for her. She seemed lost, not really a part of the conversations buzzing around the table. But for a fleeting moment everyone's attention was focused on her as she made a toast. After we had lowered our glasses, she added, almost wistfully, "Girls, aren't you all glad we graduated when we did and taught when we did?" There were a few polite murmurs and then everyone seemed to turn away. Suddenly my throat ached, and when my chicken cheese casserole arrived, I wasn't hungry. It tasted just like school paste.

And then suddenly it was over. Thirty-six years capsuled into less than three hours of dquirris, chef salads, and chicken cheese casseroles.

The house was cool and quiet when I arrived home, a note from Paul informing me that he had gone to the golf course. The drapes were drawn and the air conditioning was working again. Paul must have got it fixed after I left. I changed into a loose robe and slippers and lay down on the couch in the living room and closed my eyes. But sleep would not come. One short conversation with

Sally kept going through my mind: "It's just a lake cabin that we insulated and made into a year-round home. Please do come to see us-anytime." I hate vague invitations like that. But she did give rather specific directions.

"It's a small place," she had said. "We live very simply. Just come to the kitchen door — it's the only door." She had laughed almost apologetically. And I remembered something else. From what she said, their retirement wasn't really a retirement.

"I've got to find a secretarial job this fall," she said. There seemed a note of urgency in her voice. She added, "I don't know if anybody will hire me at my age."

"What about teaching?" I asked, knowing it was a foolish question the minute I had asked it.

"Oh, I'm too old," Sally said. "It would be too difficult to find a new teaching position with the surplus of young teachers looking for jobs." "Of course," I said. "I should have known that. It's like it was when we graduated in the depression. Remember how hard it was for us then, when we were young?" I added, wishing I could cut my tongue off. Sally hesitatingly said, "My husband is considering a position as administrator for a newly proposed private school near where we now live. We should know soon."

I sat up on the couch as I thought about those years and years of cheery Christmas messages. Sally's annual mimeographed Christmas letters, with personal messages added, never failed to ooze with an almost Pollyanna sweetness that, with the years, became increasingly irritating to me. Was it because I had started to cope with life more realistically as I gradually emerged out of my cocoon and discovered that my needs and goals in life no longer included trying to emulate Sally? Or was it that my life had had some heavy times and losses, and I resented the oh-so perfect life described in her annual messages? Her yearly recitation depicted her life as one big twinkly Christmas ornament. Everything that had happened during the past year had been "thrilling" or "very interesting" or "very educational," so many moments to be "cherished," so many "perfect" family get-togethers, so much to be "thankful" for. And as usual she ended with an uplifting sermonette. Somehow her preachments always made me feel guilty about my sundry weaknesses and less than perfect disposition. And I was so glad she couldn't see the tangle in my cupboards and checkbook.

Suddenly a thought occurred to me, and I got up from the couch and went to the chest in the hall and found the packet of cards from last Christmas. I tried to read between the cheerful lines. But there were no clues, except that the address, which had been changing almost every year, seemed to shout out that it was a very small town. And then I remembered that Paul had commented on it last Christmas.

"You're not serious," he had said. "Sally lives in Altonville?" "What's wrong with that?" I asked with some hostility. Her husband's principal of the school there."

"Altonville has a school? It's the most miserable patch of nothing, a few dreary buildings on the edge of a swamp. I know. I went through there last month on my last trip. It's Endsville, is what it is."

I only half-believed him then, because Paul does have a way of exaggerating, but now I wasn't so sure. But then I began to read between the lines. Her first and only marriage was when she was in her forties, and she had skipped from one small school to another, teaching many classes each day in various small communities. And apparently nothing had changed in all these years.

I had just barely pieced this together, when Paul came home.

"You home already?" he said, looking surprised.

"What about yourself?" I asked.

"Oh, it was much too hot. Had a couple of drinks and lunch at the club house and then went over and visited with Jack for a while."

Jack's our second oldest of three children. He's in law school. The other two are also gone. Just the two of us left. And no grandchildren.

"Well, how was Sally?" Paul asked. "Did she hold court as usual? With that beautiful blond hair, she could always capture an audience."

To my own amazement, I ran toward the open staircase. Tears streamed down my face as I ran half way up the stairs. Then I turned and looked down at Paul, who was staring at me open-mouthed.

"Her hair wasn't blond," I shouted. "It was gray. ALL GRAY."

Humor:

South Of South Is North

Things aren't always what they seem.
When I was in the fourth grade at Garfield School,
my favorite teacher, Miss Magnuson,
told the class: "If you dig deep enough,
you can reach China:

Some of the kids snickered.
Jimmy Johnson, with some help from his brother,
dug a deep hole in the front yard
and broke the water main.
His father was not pleased.
My faith in Miss Magnuson remained unbroken.

Let's look at it this way —
When you travel far enough
in the same direction,
south of south becomes north.
You know what I mean?
And, of course, east of east is west.

Say you fly east from New York to Amsterdam,
and from there continue flying in the same direction,
but just a tad southeast,
you could end up in Walla Walla, Washington.
That's about as far west as you can get,
on dry land, that is.

Of course Miss Magnuson was right.
And while there are Doubting Thomases
who insist the earth is flat
and the holocaust never happened,
there will always be the Jimmys of the world.
Inspired by the Magellans and the Miss Magnusons,
they will continue to seek new paths
to the east and to the west,
and new pathways to the planets.

A Matter Of Color

The whole silly business started back in 1953. A clever salesman cooked up a scheme to unload a surplus of lime green bath towels and took out an ad:

YOU CAN HAVE A **CHARTREUSE** BATHROOM

BE AMONG THE **FIRST** WITH THE **VERY LATEST**

It really caught on. The whole world began to turn chartreuse. Bridesmaids floated down the aisle in chartreuse organdy. Geraniums bloomed in chartreuse flower pots. Our living room was redone in - you guessed it. Even tea kettles, mixing bowls, and bumperstickers. Nothing was sacred.

Well, it didn't last long. It was the house next door that did it. Early in July the neighbors transformed their white Cape Cod with eight gallons of chartreuse latex. We all went outside to get a good look.

We stared and stared, swallowed hard as we collectively came to the same awful realization:

Chartreuse is twice as ugly as lime green.

To My Old Friend

The academic jargon you used to spew out,
my old friend,
and the cold statistics you listed
in even columns —
they belied your marshmallow heart.

My constant companion,
for years we worked together past midnight
on dreary theses,
strangers' dissertations.

The clock rushed fiendishly ahead,
knowing we were caught in a race with it.
But we'd complete it by morning,
smoothing out the tangle of yet another draft —
just in time, just in time for a frantic PHD candidate
who brought us his or her closing chapter
and appendices
one day before the deadline.

Alone together,
we'd fight the battle as the house slept.
Your keys would stick, your ribbon would fade.
I'd stamp my foot, cuss you, cuss the clock.
We would hyperventilate, the clock our mutual enemy.
Somehow we made it.
Each time we made it.

Through the years we've changed,
thesis typing days long gone.
We snub computers, word processors.
We go slowly, taste each syllable,
pause to daydream between phrases.
Sometimes words and phrases emerge mysteriously
without going through my brain at all.

I'm beginning to get wise to you, my friend.
You picked out words you liked the best
when we worked so hard together
through those early years,
stored them in your memory bank —

words of passion and beauty,
about butterflies, about young love.

We have become extensions of each other,
you and I.
We are creating poetry together,
my good old Smith Corona.

Oh Margaret!

Do you still hide
behind the counter,
Margaret,
peering out
but so afraid,
still whispering
years past your adolescence
as you issue it,
stamp life in and out,
dispense life
raw and vibrant
to those who dare?

Margaret,
you're still whispering.
I can barely hear you.
And you're growing old and frail.
They're getting much too heavy
for you to lift,
too heavy to stamp in and out.

Oh Margaret,
shy, sweet Margaret,
do you ever dare
to look at what you stamp?
Do you still blush at D. H. Lawrence?
Do you look away
as you stamp Salinger and Vonnegut?
Do you still quickly place them
alphabetically upon the shelf
as soon as they come back,
ready to be stamped out again
to those who dare?

The Crazy World Of Linguistics

Friday evening I discovered a new verb:

GENTLE

Yes, that soft, gentle word that has always been
an adjective so close to my heart.
That is, until Friday evening.

There I was, innocently dabbing Oil of Olay on my face.
I'd shake drops of Olay into the palm of my left hand,
dip into it with the tip of my right forefinger,
and literally plunk Olay onto my chin, nose, cheeks,
and forehead.

I basked in its soft, gentle tingle, certain that it
was working magic on my aging face.. I don't know
what possessed me on this particular Friday evening
to check the instructions on the bottle. After all,
I had been using it for some time.
To my amazement, right there on the bottle it now said:

"GENTLE IT ON!" "…gentle it on…?"

I saw no acknowledgement of anyone receiving permission
from Webster or from the Library of Congress or from
anyone else, for that matter, to tamper so recklessly with
such a vulnerable word. Did they even ask GENTLE if it
wanted to become a verb?

But there it was. What next? Perhaps we'll soon hear
Julia Child say, "Now we will gentle the souffle out of
the oven."

April Blizzard

Have you noticed
how things are shifting around,
speeding up,
spinning faster and faster?

Five storms of the century
in the past eighteen months.
April blizzards, June in January,
the jet stream gone mad.

We listen breathlessly—
10, 15, maybe 24 inches by nightfall.
Or will Nebraska get the whole thing,
CBS, NBC coverage?

It's picking up,
already 15 inches at the airport.
Get the snowblower, shovels ready.
Where's my red stocking cap?
These mittens don't match.
Hurry! Hurry!
Forget your scarf.
The cameras are coming!

>Published in:
>*The Lake Street Review*
>Number 19, Summer 1985

Four Eyes

*"Men never make passes
at girls who wear glasses"*
— Dorothy Parker

Years ago I envied her,
that face of Katherine Hepburn's,
those cheekbones — wow!
those eyes, that mouth
arranged above that lovely throat.

I've reconciled to what I've got,
even though it's going to pot,
even to these eyes of mine
that have peered through glasses
since I was nine.

At first I brooded about my youth,
those awful days, the 1930's,
when glasses came in "ugly" only
and all my friends saw 20/20,
and I the only girl in classes
who could not see without her glasses.

Oh, those awful days of long ago
when Dorothy Parker coined a phrase
that made me sad and made her famous
because I bought her line, and so did Hollywood.

Well, time has proved she was in error,
time to set the record straight.
Dorothy Parker has long since left us,
but we can force those movie makers
to portray a girl who **puts** on glasses,
and is SUDDENLY so **very** BEAUTIFUL!

Star Dust

Now that we have come of age
and learned how to tell it like it is,
exactly where are we?
I tried hard,
cut off my Shirley Temple curls years ago,
abandoned my dream to be a Hollywood star.
But isn't it getting a bit tiresome?
I never could wear jeans,
or call a spade a spade.
Family togetherness, encounter groups
are mostly yesterday's news.
The kids got married,
moved to the East Coast.

Have you noticed that satin and velvet are back,
and high heels?
Big band sound. Star Dust.
If I were younger taller thinner
I'd wear my hair just like Greta Garbo did —
long, blonde pageboy falling over one eye.
Cultivate that husky voice. That Profile.
Amazing what you can do with shadows
and the right lighting.
The effect, darling, the effect!

Translations from the Finnish:

Author's Recitals
At FinnFest '92,

Duluth, Minnesota
July 25, 1992

A poem (in translation from the Finnish):
Translated by Aili Jarvenpa

Minä kuulin naisten laulavan
(I heard women singing)

Written by Arvo Turtiainen, often called the grand old man of Finnish poetry. A central figure in left-wing literature, he fought for his country in the Winter War and was wounded, but was imprisoned as a pacifist during the Continuation War. He was born in 1904, and died in 1980.

Minä kuulin naisten laulavan,
    lukemattomien naisäänien,
    jokaisen omalla tavallaan.

I heard women singing -
    countless numbers of women's voices,
    each one in her own way.

They sang beside hearths in their homes,
    beside cradles
and while resting between chores.

I heard women singing,
    each one in her own way.
Old women sang to their sons
    whom the war had taken away

and to their husbands
    whom work had broken.
Their singing was as wise and as sad
    as their fate.

I heard women singing,
    each in her own way.
Young women sang of their strength
    in which they had faith
or of their children, whose future
    with its hard journeys, they could see.

I heard women singing
    each according to her own heart.
Young women sang of love
    which would come
    or already had arrived.
Early morning was in their voices
    the rising sun in the words of their songs.

I heard women singing
    freely and with deepest emotion
about everything in their lives that they loved
    and in their dreams that they believed
And I became aware of hearing that
    which I never before had heard.

I heard women singing
    and realized that my own life
    was being sung by their voices
It was life's cradle song to myself
    and a song of love to my fate.
It was a song of dedication
    a blessing of courage

I heard women singing
    and I became aware that
    through me they were singing for everyone.

"Silver and Violet," by Eeva Kilpi,
from her collection,
ennen kuolemaa (Before Death),
WSOY, 1982, p. 33.

Translated by Aili Jarvenpa

Silver and Violet

The weather is getting warmer now,
that is how I am sad.
A poem comes only after a person is totally exhausted
and hardly has strength to write it.
It has been a big day.
My children here after a long absence,
and I: melancholy and happy that they were here,
their attention — that they treated me well
and I them, so that the reunion did succeed;
I feel I have done a good job
— and now I rejoice with their departure, that they have
their own lives from which they can come to greet
my life
and me here, as you would a snow tiger.
My thoughts are so old today,
very old,
like those dressed in silver and violet
and gray silk
and the light hurts so, hurts so.

Poem by Eeva Kilpi

Translated by Aili Jarvenpa

Life's Refugee

I loved you as I loved Karelia,
I loved you as I loved summer,
I loved you as I loved my father and mother,
I loved you as I loved my children.

I cried for you as I cried for Karelia,
I cried for you as I cried for my home,
I cried for you as I cried for that boy
who promised but never did come.

I laughed then as I laughed in Karelia,
I laughed then as I laughed as a child,
I laughed then as I laughed with that girl
who chose me from everyone else.

I remember you as I remember Karelia,
I remember you as I remember Christmas,
I remember you as I remember that special path
that perhaps never was there.

I hear that the trees there still bear leaves,
I hear that the birches still grow,
and the cuckoos still sing there, I have heard
— and why should it not be so?

And autumn there still takes the leaves away
and winter covers with white,
and the cuckoos still fly from there to the south
and the flowers die under the ice.

I loved you then, do you hear, do you hear,
and I guess that I love you still,
while I, a life's refugee,
continue to wander throughout the world.

Poem by Eeva Kilpi

Translated by Aili Jarvenpa

Chance

If nothing else,
chance protects us.
In the same way it protects
mating butterflies
from the wind and human feet,
even though, because of our deeds, we are
less worthy than they.
Butterflies mate for an hour or more
and it's amazing they are not trampled,
amazing that birds don't eat them
or the wind take them
although it's windy
or the rain doesn't separate or beat them down
although it rains.
They quiver but remain together
on a blade of grass.
Chance does not make a difference.
Something always succeeds.
Butterflies have multiplied.
It may go well for other things too.
Depression, despair, a wavering of your mind
do not change anything for the worse.
Nothing is so terribly significant.
Nothing.
When you learn that, it is easier
whether you are of the same opinion or not.

Translated by Aili Jarvenpa

poem, *"Morsiamet"*
by Eeva Kilpi, in *ennen kuolemaa,*
(Before Death), WSOY, 1982.

The Brides

1
Planes fly. Guns fire.
The world speaks with the voice it has.
But the bride stands in the snow in her small shoes
and lights a candle in the ice lantern
under the new moon.
Walls radiate. We hug. We kiss.
Happiness, happiness,
eyes well with tears.
Everyone loves the bride.
The dying lift their faces toward her.

2
Immediately after the wedding,
when the groom returns to his garrison,
the mass media announces the decision has been made
to begin construction of the neutron bomb.
It annihilates the living — as you know —
but saves the inanimate.
It destroys vermin in hand-me-down furniture
but saves the wedding gifts and the groom's rifle,
leaves the photographs to look at each other
and keeps the bride's smile.
Technology builds itself a museum of its dreams.
The public is eliminated.
Perfection is finally achieved.
From now on it is unnecessary to strive for it.
Nervous coughing,
irrelevant questions,
dirty feet
no longer disturb the order.

3
Don't worry: the bride is smiling.
Right above her stomach is a cloud of small angels,
and glitter rains down from her eyes onto her breasts.
With four hands she lifts the church roof
for new winds to come,
and relatives on both sides of the entrance
drink hope.
Look at the bride's face, world, and
read your fate from it as the groom does.
Don't worry as long as the bride is smiling.
She knows.
She is pregnant with joy.
She is light from strength.
She is firm and fearless in her beauty.
She has enough to create the world.
Don't worry: the bride is smiling.

4
The earth is so beautiful.
The earth is so beautiful in order to make it
difficult to lose it,
to make us sad when it is destroyed.
It defends itself with its beauty.
It looks us in the eye and asks:
How can anything destroy me?
Nature grows to avoid death.
Growth is the only power against destruction.
Also beauty.
When the development of weapons has reached its ultimate,
and nothing can become more deadly,
beauty rises against destruction
stronger than ever before,
stronger than anyone has ever risen.
Nothing can stand up against beauty.
In front of beauty, weapons are powerless.

5
The bride is smiling.
There is nothing more beautiful than a bride's smile.
From her eyes glitter falls down upon her breasts,
right above her stomach a small cloud hovers.
She smiles victorious
and carries our future step by step

closer to us.
Against all anguish, all pain and threats,
the bride steps, smiling.
A soldier's vow now meaningless, we stop being afraid,
and soon the child kicks for the first time.
The bride is smiling.
She knows without knowing:
it may go differently,
it may go well.

The bride is smiling.
In front of her smile, weapons are lowered.
Her smile will not fade.
The bride's smile is unconditional.
It answers every moment: I do.

6
The youngest bride dances.
She has only recently stepped out of her child's shoes
but already looks a bit like a wife
as she turns at the altar, a ring on her finger.
And the groom, like a blackbird snared
in her whiteness, dances with her.
Who leads and who follows
when love, like a beautiful prey,
speeds them across the floor's meadow?

Dance, youngest bride, dance.
As long as you dance
there is hope,
as long as you dance
the world has the strength to believe and love.
May you shed your virginity slowly
so the world won't grow old.
It is young with you.
It is young as long as you dance,
a ryeflower in your hair.
Seeds of birches rain down
and the youngest bride dances,
shoes of her childhood abandoned,
and her maidenhood, with the tinge of a wife,
sheds slowly.
And the world dreams.
Its heart fluttering, it bows to you like a groom

and hopes to be accepted.
Youngest bride, dance with the world,
twirl it until it's exhausted, youngest bride.
The youngest bride dances her sisters into mutual
                understanding,
brothers as brothers to each other.
She has just been freed from a child's shoes
and already turns at the altar, looking a bit like a wife.
There is not much time.
Therefore dance, youngest bride.
The world loves you the most.
For your sake, the world doesn't want to die.
Dance, youngest bride.
There is no worry while the bride is dancing.

7
The last one to step to the altar is the serious bride
and she also says: — I do.
A wreath of roses in her hair, she wants autumn and winter
just as before
and after autumn and winter, spring
and early summer and summer,
mid-summer and continuity.
Thus the brides step forward wanting for us
the seasons of the year one after the other.
The corner of her mouth quivering a bit, the serious bride
gives her promise.
Her hip sways slightly inside the white gown
remembering its strength,
and despair flutters aside.

The unwed sit
peacefully around,
unhurried, trusting.

This is what life wants.
Life wants it like this.
A charming challenge
before death.

Poetry and Prose:

Bay Islands, Honduras

The Taormina

February 1980

You knew where to find the sweetest in life
as only those who sail the TAORMINA know.
You brought us to the Bay Islands,
five Nordic descendants from frozen waters,
Lake Bemidji, Lake Nokomis, Puulavesi.
And we sailed with you, Arvi,
white sails aloft,
holding high the blue of the sky,
south winds lifting our spirits
above the Caribbean,
high above the coral reefs.

Out of Port Royal Harbor we sailed,
out from the ancient hideaway of buccaneers,
past the lush green hills of Roatan Island,
on to Guanaja where Columbus once came.
On the TAORMINA we sailed,
the sun's rays warming our northern faces.

We sail with you now, Arvi,
across blue waters,
across all barriers,
to an island warmed by a new radiance.

— For Arvi who died Christmas Eve 1980

Inner City High School
(In the 1960's)

I

Angry Afro-American girl of the 'sixties,
born in white man's city,
long in white man's big city
streets and schools,
Angry Afro-American girl with white man's
history book,
How many ways have we taught you to fear us,
to hate us,
Angry Afro-American girl?

Only once did I see you lower your guard.
Only once did I hear you speak softly.
"Teacher," you said,
"Your dreams can come true. Mine never will."

I had no easy answers that day.

II

Shy young Native American boy new to white man's city,
new to white man's big city streets,
big city schools,
to its unfamiliar clocks and gongs
and bells,
Shy young Native American boy labeled "savage"
in white man's history book,
White man who took away your land, your rights,
your self worth.

How many ways did we teach you to fear us,
Shy young Native American boy?
I remember the day you skipped class.
Eyes glued to your shoes, you whispered,
"Teacher, I got real sick and had to go puke."

Did we defeat you,
Shy young Native American boy?
I believe you have grown strong with your brothers,
Shy young Native American boy, and
Today, as a man, you hold your head high.

Dance Of The Snowshoe Hares

*"A little longer will make him
so white we shall not see him
in the whitened trees."*
— from Yevtushenko's *"Schoolmaster"*

The full moon weaves its lunar magic
in the stillness of the winter night,
and the snowshoe hares,
captured by the spell,
emerge from the safety of their spruce bog
to dance a ghostly dance of madness,
an ageless dance of rapture
in the forest night.

Bewitched, they frolic in the moonlight,
dance and chase each other
up and down their snowy runways,
up and down converging trails,
black eyes glistening as they dance
within the orbit of the moon,
protected by their winter fur
whitened for the winter,
protected by the whitened runways
within the whitened forest.

But one young foolish hare,
overcome by the sphere of silver,
leaps boldly into open meadow
and becomes the hunted.
His tracks, no longer hidden by the trees
but illumined by his moon,
circle snow drifts,
leap fences dividing whitened fields,
then head back in desperate leaps
toward the forest, toward the trees,
where his tracks finally vanish
as he whitens into white like the trees.
Soon we shall not see him
in the whitened trees.

For Sigurd F. Olson

Published in:
Storystone, Winter 1980,
and in
**Storystone,
A Retrospective,**
Summer 1982

Three Years

Wars are tailor made for brides and grooms,
to toughen them, to test their love,
with fragile threads of censored letters
from the ancient Nile to Lake Nokomis,
from pine-scented forests to the Libyan Desert,
rich with the stench of G.I. mutton aging in the sun,
from London under siege to sheltered Minneapolis.

Life in limbo
hemispheres apart,
with censored letters precariously connecting
when the war permits.
Dreams suspended, hanging in mid air,
perhaps forever.

Wars are tailor made for brides and grooms
to toughen them, to test-their love,
to fear
to weep
to flail at loneliness
to hide the wedding gifts
to write a letter to wash my hair
to wash my hair to write a letter
to wait for mail to wait for mail
to search the headlines for hope not there
     DIRECT BOMB HITS IN THE LIBYAN DESERT
to wait
to write a letter
to wait
to search the headlines
     NAZI ROMMEL, DESERT FOX, VICTORIOUS IN TUNISIA
to wait   to wait
to search the headlines
     BUZZ BOMBS SMASH LONDON

to wait
D-Day . . . Normandy Beach . . . Battle of the Bulge

to wait
     Rheims . . . . Luxembourg . . . . Liege
     Hitler on the run . . . . HITLER ON THE RUN

TO WAIT . . . TO WAIT
    MUNICH . . . ERLANGEN . . . . NUREMBERG

to wait
    boston
    boston, massachusetts
    columbus day 1945
    o holy christopher columbus day

El Salvador
February 6, 1982   **News Bulletin**

*"reserved for itself
the most succulent...
the delicate waist of America."*
— Pablo Neruda

Children are dying in El Salvador.
It is easy to die here,
this small mountainous country
squeezed between Honduras and the Pacific.
Advisors and reporters fly in daily,
the civil war suddenly the whole world's business.

Spanish conquistadors once knew this land,
met the Indians.
Their blood now mingles.
Today, forces and counter forces are more complex.
Or are they?

Do you see the children huddling together,
eyes glued to our cameras?
Their mothers continue to hang their daily wash
in front of our cameras,
in the very center of war.
Routine of living is the only sanity left.

Children are dying in El Salvador,
white wash billowing above them.
Even dogs are afraid.
Silent, bony, they slink under bushes.
Only at night do they howl.

The tongue of death is near.
Parrots screech in the jungle.

Kate Millett

With soft voice,
you speak for those of us
who dare not speak,
sisters bonded by a hope
long lost in shadow.

You speak for us
who are veiled in silence,
who claim nothing in our names,
not our birth rights,
the children we have borne,
not mother's milk flowing rich,
the earth saturated with our sorrow.

You lead us, march with us,
mothers, daughters,
within the shadow of their guns,
expose one by one
their chains of power,
centuries of oppression
evoked in God's name.

With soft clear voice
you free us from darkness.

My No Longer Child

My youngest,
my no longer child,
I measure this new aging in your eyes,
this new presence I have yet to know.

I touch the soft curve
of your young face
and long to hold you as a child again.
But your eyes warn me
not to break your strength.

The Spruce

                At Kangasniemi, Finland
                August 8, 1978

The old house is gone
like you said, Father,
but the dark spruce stands tall,
spreading its green
above the lonely field,
empty barn.

If I had the voice, Father,
I would tell you how it is for me,
always knowing of this home
named Puusteli,
yet standing here for the first time
beside the tree you planted as a child.

It is so tall now.
It holds the summer sky filled with rain.
We weep together of that time
when your only hope was in its growing.

Its roots go far, as far as yours,
into the soil,
the rocky hills of Kangasniemi,
to birds calling their lament,
deep to Arctic winds, to the core of hunger.
They go back to an August day like this,
when, at eighteen, you said goodbye
and left alone
for a place called Minnesota.

Yes, Father, it is tall now,
and its wide branches reach far, far
across the waters and the darkness,
the wind-whipped sky,
to a new warmth and light.

Hymn To The Moon Goddess

o goddess moon o mother of life
i lift my eyes up toward your light
i play for you my willow flute
my spring-time flute of supple willow
o goddess moon o mother of life
i play for you this young spring night

that you will shed the waters down
to quench the earth
to touch the seeds
to bring new life fertility
o goddess moon o crescent of light
i play for you this young spring night

but withhold your flooding storms of August
o goddess moon of rain and darkness
o goddess moon of love and harvest
i play for you my willow flute
i honor you this young spring night

moon goddess
        rain goddess
                mother of life

Dream Of Aging

I have arrived,
afraid,
at this place
where there are no names.
Old labels
fade
one by one
as the grayness
encloses.

I reach upward,
wave my credentials
toward
those in charge.
They approach
stiff-uniformed,
pat me on the head
and murmur
"there, there."

I grow invisible.

A Way Of Looking At The Sun

There is a way of looking at the sun
                              that is safe
That is, not to look at it at all
but, rather, at the light that shines softly
through maple leaves, flickers gently
on the pond below, or on your face
as you turn smiling in answer to my call

There is a way of looking into your eyes
                              that is safe
That is, not to look into them at all
but, rather, into their reflection
in the pond as they move
with the rippling of the water,
smiling first at me,- and then away

Arctic Terns

How is it
that the Arctic Terns,
so small,
can wing their way
from pole to pole
and back each year
and always find the places
they call home,

While you and I,
with maps and guides
from triple A,
are confused
by clearly labeled
exit ramps
and head for Jersey
when our destination
is the Bronx?

Invitation
To
Reunion

It threads
a long path
through
velvet ribbons of rivers
darkest ribbons of night

Persistently trails me
through
roses of red
red roses of fire
winter's long shadows
dreams dead or dying

This mist
its sweet scent
reaches out
through the years
through decades of summers
old letters
lost years

It stalks me
through wars
the births
of my children

This mist
from the past
knows
just how to find me

Reaches out
beckons me

And I answer
    yes I will come
        yes I will come

From Helsinki to Kennedy Airport

I had just attended a women's conference in Helsinki, called "Reunion of Sisters." For me it had been an incredible gathering of women writers, women professors, women doctors, women teachers, women members of parliament, all reaching out to each other, learning from each other, studying world issues, issues at home.

But now it was time for us Americans to head for home. We boarded a beautiful ship in the Helsinki harbor named Silja Line. As we sailed, I saw the most beautiful sunset that I had ever seen. We arrived in Stockholm the next morning, and were then driven to the airport for our flight home.

Our plane was on time, the meals on the flight the best I'd ever had on any flight, and the staff at our beck and call.

How perfect everything was, I thought. Little did I know what was going to happen somewhat later. Everything was going so well, and I had my good friend Doris with me, and we were having a great time.

Our arrival at Kennedy Airport was somewhat hectic, as usual, what with being a half hour late and the airport being unusually crowded. In less than ten minutes Doris and I lost each other. I managed to get through customs, but no sign of Doris. I went to wait for my luggage, then suddenly realized I was in the wrong place. Eventually I found the desk where I presented my ticket to fly from Kennedy to the Minneapolis Airport.

Then came my worst nightmare: I lost my purse. Yes, my big gray-colored purse with my cash, my credit cards, my keys — all that and more in it. I didn't even have a quarter to phone anyone. And no sign of Doris.

I started going toward the ticket desk, when I heard a voice calling my name. I turned around and saw a tall woman standing next to where the luggage is examined. I ran toward her. Smiling, she asked, "Is this yours?" holding up my gray purse. "Yes," I said, and started to cry. "Don't cry, honey," the tall woman said, "Everything's all right."

P.S. Doris and I finally found each other when we arrived at the Minneapolis airport.

Day Of Reckoning

I have been actively sedentary most of my life. I break out in hives when I hear words like "aerobics," "gymnastics." A slow foxtrot has suited me just fine, or a stroll to the mailbox. Even as a child, my favorite sport was carrying books home from our small town Carnegie library, stopping along the way for a hot fudge sundae at Raiter's Drugstore.

Back in those days, the twenties and thirties, dairy products and three big meals a day were what made you healthy, wealthy and wise — and fat. But not me. I was as skinny as a rail through it all, even though I obeyed the daily threat, "Eat every bit on your plate — or else."

I confess. I did engage in one real sport. When I was nine, I would roller skate along Fourteenth Street with great speed. But I got no recognition whatsoever. Fourteenth Street in Cloquet went down a steep hill, so all the kids went fast.

In 1937, as a student in Duluth Junior College, I had the dubious distinction of setting the lowest record in girls' high jump — I missed the lowest setting. However, being female and non-athletic was no big deal in those days. The important thing was to try to look like Carole Lombard. Only Lorna Johnson in my English class came even close. And I didn't have to compare my daily jogging record with anyone. Nobody jogged back then. Nor did I count the number of laps I could do in the swimming pool. Our college didn't have a pool.

Sixty years of being actively sedentary didn't prepare me for the 1980's. By 1981 I had even given up foxtrotting. But then the barrage started. It was everywhere, the campaign to reduce heart disease, heart attacks. DIET EXERCISE EXERCISE DIET CHOLESTEROL CALORIES HDL LDL. New findings. New medications. It became a chant, a constant drumming on television, radio, in the newspapers, magazines. I tried to ignore it although I was at least 25 pounds overweight, and first signs of angina had started. I had my little bottle of nitroglycerin pills in my purse wherever I went. At the first twinge of pain or difficulty breathing, I would pop a pill under my tongue, and in less than a minute feel just great.

In January 1982 I had my heart attack — right in the downtown Minneapolis library. The paramedics came. They looked like spacemen. I was told it was a "mild" attack. After a few days I was sent home with a newly discovered "miracle" drug, a calcium blocker. It did seem miraculous. It lulled me into a false security. Before long I forgot about dieting, skipped my exercises. The day of reckoning came. October 8, 1985. The voice of the cardiologist was not unkind, but firm, unrelenting. "I'm sorry. There are no easy outs for you. New pills, new diets are now as useless as bandaids. No, angioplasty won't work in your case. You're way past that. The angiogram shows four clogged arteries, two of them 100 percent. They are killing you. By-pass surgery is your **only** option."

Ten years have gone by. I know I am very lucky. Yet memories of months of recuperation fade slowly, and I find myself getting into old patterns, walking only when I go shopping, sneaking bites of forbidden foods. I blush when caught ("It was just a small piece"). I still breathe freely, but if I hear the word "angina" I remember the old pain.

Her *Laulu*

As a child I heard her singing,
lovely voice so clear and haunting,
singing memories of her childhood
for which she pined and lamented
of the old days she then chanted,
of youth and dreams both now vanished
in the land of lakes and birches.

Now I chant, I sing her *laulu,*
song of love, her song of yearning,
and I long for lakes and birches
and the home she always ached for,
so far away in the northland
the summer sun, it shines forever,
warms the heart for winter's darkness,
her lovely *laulu,* song of love.

—In memory of my mother

NORMANDALE COMMUNITY COLLEGE
LIBRARY
9700 FRANCE AVENUE SOUTH
BLOOMINGTON, MN 55431-4399